Relationships
with Everything and Everyone

By William Linville

Acknowledgements

This book about relationships with everyone and everything has been a long time awaited and coming. It's about how to let relationships work, how to let them grow, how to let them become you, how to let them take on their own life, how to let them be a life force within themselves. It's about a constant camaraderie, beside you and around you and also a relationship with oneself: A self that has so many facets, a self that takes so many twists and turns and a self, that first and foremost, matters the most; a self that takes on a life of its own, that continues to grow and expand upon itself, becoming quite integrated and quite strong within itself as it is constantly changing within itself, flourishing, but never again closing and turning on itself, no longer battling itself.

This book is about relationships of great enjoyment, great ease and divine simplicity as you let them begin to work with ease and simplicity. It is about how to be a guide within them at times, and at other times, just being able to enjoy them and step back, to watch how they grow without all the push and the pulls, all the combativeness involved and without the necessity of: Who's right? Who's wrong? Who needs to be right?

Who needs to be the carrier? Who needs to be the caretaker? Relationships do not happen just by chance and they give to you as you are mutually giving to them.

This book is about how to let relationships open and take on the life that they were always meant to be, in every way, within every situation, with every object, within every level of life. As relationships begin to work for you and as you honor the dear ones before you, watch how quickly your relationships spontaneously come to life and you affect everyone else involved.

I dedicate this book to my wife, my best friend, my partner, my divine radiant bride, My Angel; Mary Elizabeth Linville, who is the most priceless, angelic presence - a relationship that takes no work, that has a life of its own and that we celebrate and enjoy passionately, exquisitely and divinely side-by-side. For all that they've put into the beautiful creation of this book, all their priceless transcribing, editing and all the love that they've put into this book, this book is also dedicated to Mike and Jennifer Connell, who are two such beautiful, divine, radiant facets of their own; to Becci and Bruce Christensen and all the love, diligent work and editing that they have put into this book; to Joe Palermo, who has done an overseeing of reading and giving input; to Deb Bohn who has also done reading and offered input to My Angel's chapter. The love that each of these dear ones has added to this book has also put that love into you and all the lives that are being changed by this book.

This book is dedicated to all of humanity that are looking and searching for ways to let relationships work for themselves and work for the whole. It is dedicated to everyone that's ever been such a priceless assistance to Universalis, Inc.; Sally O'Brien, Dale Sutton, all of the beautiful dear ones that I have personally had the great honor of dancing with and walking with in the priceless relationships that we have had and that we do have; to all the dear ones that have come in and out of our life-streams, of relationship of connecting, creating and then moving forth, of a priceless, Universal dance as relationships were created to be - to not hold on, but to mutually honor side-by-side. And then, last but not least this book is dedicated to the whole Universe entirely, that it's forever encompassing and embracing each and every one of us as well as you.

The Universe is constantly sharing with us: *We would love to speak with you and give to you, to hold you and to embrace you as the beautiful family, the beautiful omnipotence, the beautiful presence that you are. We would love to steer you, journey you, share and offer you so much more than what your mental and emotional levels ever could have, and could ever even fathom to create.*

So as you let the Universe, through the covers of this book, begin to take you on a journey through you, into you, and all around you into your life as a whole, it is a passageway of letting the Universe carry you, lift you up, lift you into you and also embrace you; embrace you as the most important relationship there is - the relationship with all that is - you embodying and being embraced by and with your Creator consciousness, which is letting you be embraced and be loved as the beloved Incarnate that you are.

I know you will enjoy yourself, as you are welcomed into your relationship with yourself.

Namaste'

Table of Contents

Acknowledgements iii

Introduction ix

Let's Begin with Clarity 1

Who You Are 11

*A True Loving Relationship of the Heart
with Your Life-Stream, Your Beingness
and the Whole Universe* 23

*A True Loving Relationship of the Heart
with Another* 37

*Excellent Questions Asked by
Many Dear Ones* 47

*William and Mary's Relationship of the Heart
Questions & Answers* 69

*Our Relationship of the Heart – Questions
Asked by Many Dear One* 72

In Closing 101

Appendix A 103

Appendix B 107

Introduction

This book has been created and designed for all concerned. No matter where you are on your journey you will be able to begin to grasp the clarity and fluidity of the light-beingness, the love that you are. Some of the material in this book is going to be beyond the mind's level of understanding with the first analytical reading. As you continue to read through, you will find that the mind will begin to absorb and open to all of the accessibility and information that is available for you, for as it is a marriage of the mind and the heart to begin to let all relationships with everything and everyone begin to work, improve and come to life.

You will begin to see your life-stream moving forth from you and for you as you read through this book and address and play with the mental level, the constructs of the mental level, as well as your higher levels, lower levels, causal levels, emotional levels, the psyche, the sub-psyche, etc. For some, reading this is going to begin to create a lot of questioning of oneself. The questions are going to create answers from so many different planes and levels that the mental states may not fully grasp all of the content and may attempt to pull you back from your heart level; yet all is well. Answers come forth from questions and it is important to give the mental and emotional levels a certain level of clarity and understanding so you can begin to run forth to all that is available for you; and as the mind is your friend, there are examples for the mind level to use so it can fully step right in, to see what truly is, as you go right back into the heart level and move forth even faster and easier. There are many activations happening for you throughout this transcript that is a journey of you letting everything inside of you, and outside of you, begin to work harmoniously as it is and was created. So let's enjoy this divine journey together.

Let's Begin with Clarity

This book will steer you into you; into your clarity to find oneself within every particle of creation, letting the particles of creation come into total and complete alignment to take you beyond everything you have experienced in a body on a planet and to bring you fully and completely through being in a body on a planet, into all that is; letting your whole life-stream become completely receptive to all that is.

When it comes to relationships, let's not have any limitations nor confinements. This book will provide you clarity about yourself and your relationship within your own beingness that is healthy, whole and complete. It will also provide you clarity in a wholeness of a relationship with another, from an intimate loving relationship of the heart through openness, solidification, fluidity and communion of a relationship of the heart, with your life-stream and with the whole Universe itself.

Let's welcome in the beautiful dear ones that further complement you on every level of creation, whether it be business, family or personal. You already complement them just by your divine presence showing up around them; and as you go on your journey through all your relationships with dear ones, let's not be *one with everyone on the planet* so that you don't become polarized. Let's let everything be in a fluidity state without the necessity of abrasiveness, without any; *I am going within, I am going outside of myself, or I am looking outside of myself,* or with any of the mental, emotional vacillations or creating something to be about a self that is not a self; a self that is a false self that was taught and repeated to be about you, that has nothing to do with you, that has been shown, has been repeated and has been ingrained and embedded within your mind, your emotions and your consciousness, from an in-depth embeddedness that has been perceived about you. This book will steer you into you letting your whole life-stream, the Universe, the outside world, the body, the mind and you come together, work and flow together.

The meaning of fluidity here is that when dynamic situations and relationships are offered, you are addressing them and walking through them, but you are not becoming overtaken by the people or situations being presented, nor overtaking them. You are not planting your metaphoric feet in the ground, nor drawing lines in the sand, nor playing the *I am so powerful game,* to force a certain outcome to take place and all this kind of stuff. You are addressing and playing with the dynamics unfolding around you and letting everything work together for you so that it can flourish to complement you.

For any dear brothers whose mind struggles with this material and at the same time may be feeling that you should keep reading and listening and that there is something here for you, even if the mind cannot quite comprehend or see how what is being shared here is possible, for the comfortability of the mind, let's acknowledge that the mind is looking for something that is very concrete. It is looking for a set of *How-To-s* with *Steps 1, 2, 3, 4, 5.* The mind only knows what it's been taught. The mind is your friend and partner, yet it is not you. The mind, as a tool, is being expanded here, to be stretched and lose its grasp as you are now looking at so much more, with such broader clarity and letting the mind come along to catch up and open further, to begin to see all that is beyond a confined singular facet of an identity.

There are many different forms of the mind/intellect. There are intellects that are staunch, intellects that are rigid, intellects that are divine, intellects that are open, intellects that are withdrawn, intellects that are black and white, intellects that are multicolored, etc. As you read this, it is a beautiful uncoiling of the intellect. Expect not to understand every facet of the stream of consciousness, or the uncoiling of your mind, your DNA, RNA and of everything that you ever experienced in a body on a planet. The intellect cannot put anything based in love, particles of light consciousness, particles of Creator Consciousness into a locked-in, format-able structure, nor into a locked-in box. There are a lot of formulas for the mind to put information into a box and yet, there is not one accurate formula to put what is being shared here within a box.

And, right here, right now, feel what is happening in the frontal lobe of your brain. Let's look upon and within every facet of creation around you right now. Let's feel all the peeling away of everything and the removal of what is being peeled away of everything that you have ever felt, seen, experienced, or been taught about the topic of a relationships and the topic of you. From here, you may attempt to gain an understanding of the material, of what your body is experiencing, etc. Understanding is beautiful because it creates clarity, wisdom, freedom and assists one to move forward and yet, at the same time, it is not necessary. So for the sake of understanding, you are stepping into a new world. You could call it the real world. You will call it the world you have been waiting for; the world that you have been feeling and remembering is possible, the world you have been welcoming forth, and at the same time, it is the world many have been very afraid of for many reasons, including fear of the unknown or the perceptional lack of a purpose or direction.

As you are going through many changes right now and beginning to explore this new world - your true world, your natural world - to have a taste of what it is like to have you, to have this priceless opportunity to watch what happens around you and for you, for your life-stream, I have a favor to ask where the intellect is concerned: Don't believe what you are reading and what is being shared.

Let's put this book down, right here and now for 72 hours and expect nothing in your day-to-day life. Let's watch everything that is happening around you and through you. Let's get up, do what you do, go about your daily activities without changing a thing. As you go throughout your day just watch and don't do anything about what is occurring other than watching. Make sure you watch the changes that are going on within you and your body. You are not going to celebrate, nor not celebrate. You are just going to watch what is occurring. You will go on with your day-to-day interactions and activities without changing anything or fixing anything. Just watch [1] for 72 linear hours. Just watch what happens within you, your body principle and the outside world. Watch what is moving in and what is moving out, what is appearing within your life-stream and disappearing within your life-stream, without you being in charge of it. After the 72 hours, come back and continue reading, or should I say continue unfolding. This is not trivial. This is not a story about the three bears and Goldilocks. This is about your life-stream, your whole world. Please take everything lightly, because nothing should be serious, and please remember this is about you. In letting your life-stream take on its own life, you are free to step into your own knowingness and surpass everything that has ever been taught that could possibly confine you.

First and foremost, I honor everyone's teachings. All teachings on this planet have been divinely orchestrated, taught and given. There have been so many dear brothers that have been stepping into their natural birthright and stepping into so many different parameters and different unfoldments of the so many

---

[1] Appendix A: The Difference Between Watching and Observing

different facets of their own life-streams, in so many different forms, attributes, directions and diverse levels of clarity that are so heartfelt and honored.

Some have been sharing about abundance and how to create. Some have been sharing about the physicality and how to let it arise using different modalities. All has been divinely orchestrated and inspired. This information has been giving humanity back its power, one step after another. It has been giving dear brothers the courage to step beyond where they have been, to step beyond the need to be with another and depend on another's happiness to have your own, to enjoy and flourish in your life as never before. How many beautiful writings have there been about following your heart and you will find success and the joy you have been seeking? How many different writings have there been on being your light-beingness because light attracts light and dark attracts dark?

Doesn't it seem like there are so many truths on this planet? How about you begin to step into your own knowingness? Let's begin to unravel all the truths from where dear brothers have been and let's begin to unravel all the filtrations that have been put upon you, put into you, embodied by you. Let's begin to explore your own divine gifts. For even as we share within this writing, let's honor you first and foremost. Let's honor your courageousness to explore your own birthright within your heart, within all of your complete knowingness, using your words. Let's honor your own journey here; the journey of the pathway of your heart, your light-beingness beyond the egoic structure, mental levels and the emotional states, etc.

For as you are going through these portals beyond questioning oneself, to stepping into oneself, you are letting your love, your light-beingness and natural birthrights show and expose themselves. So let yourself have the courage to have everything; for as you grow and have the willingness and courage to open and no longer settle for what has always been and you go beyond the locked-in ideological approaches, you step into all that is and the realms of *show me more*. Remember, what is put forth in front of you is in your highest and best good and you are more than ready for it and have been waiting for it.

Now when it comes to myself, everything that I'm steering and journeying, singing and dancing and playing with, offering for all of brother humanity; yes, I am we'll call it *facilitating, assisting, guiding and journeying*; but it all is about you. You see, everything I share, everything I assist with, everything I facilitate and sing and dance and flourish with, well all, completely, thoroughly, totally, innately, is all about you stepping into you.

You see I don't consider myself a teacher. I don't consider myself a guide. I don't even consider myself a facilitator. I am who I am. I am Creator Incarnate. You can call me spirit incarnate. I am already thoroughly married with my *big guns*[2] because I am my *big guns*. I'm not a William.

---

[2] Your family; entourage, guides, angelic, archangelic, ascended host realms

I'm not *A Way* and all this fun stuff. I am who I am. This book is not about a William. It's about a you; about playing translucently, openly, exquisitely, but most importantly singing and dancing and playing with you. You see you are your own following. I'm not looking for anything to gain or lose because as far as I'm concerned, it all just is; but boy am I having a blast overtime, reminding you and assisting you to step into you, with nothing held back, nothing withdrawn; *Hey bring it on, let's go.* Because now, taking all these colorful mental and emotional justifications, dynamics and all this silly stuff out of it, well wow, this is you stepping into you; and how best can I remind you? How best can I dance with you? How best can I walk with you, clearing the deck, singing and dancing, flourishing overtime?

As you start to bypass all the colorful dynamics that have been playing out around you, you supersede them. You evolve from them. You expand beyond them, because all of the colorful dynamics are occurring to steer you back to you overtime, and to best assist you to flourish; then you start to take the different facilitations and work and then wow, you remember there's nothing that can hold you back or affect yourself; and then you start to go beyond all of that, to start to come to terms with nothing but nothing can get in your way, because nothing has the ability to get in your way, nothing has the ability to take you over. You are not subservient to anyone or anything. Then you go beyond that, to beginning to become the facilitator, to beginning to become the guide and then starting to play with yourself, starting to play with all your entourages/presences around you. You even start to go into full circle, and quite divinely speaking, the facilitator of facilitators, of the whole within your own mastery of the whole, as you're singing and dancing, flourishing quite exquisitely, quite dynamically to being that of a conduit of assistance, of creativity and Creator Incarnate and letting creation start to work for you. So let yourself go into what works for you, what calls to you and who you are, because that's really the purpose of all the opportunities, journeys and journeyers that are presented to you.

Who You Are

Who you are has many diversified multi-facets. You are Creator Incarnate. You're a Creator of all that is, not just the Creator of your Universe, not just the Creator of your reality, you're the Creator of all that is; Creator overseeing all the un-manifest, the un-manifest particles of consciousness before particles were ever segregated and separated. Before particles were ever segregated, you were a mass, a mass of a wholeness that was just one beautiful conglomerate of light-beingness. Light being that of particles of gold, which was the only fabrication that was; one beautiful mass of a solidified collective of many particles of pure light before it began to segregate upon itself, even beginning to contemplate upon itself to begin creating upon itself, to begin to experience and express itself.

Imagine drawing 93 zillion, 843 billion, 993 million, 784 thousand and 971 hundred little dots. These dots are cylindrical particles. You could call the conglomerate of these particles *Creator Consciousness or Creator Particles,* and when you break that up into all these little particles of *Goldlets* - call that a *Gold Collective* - a collective that was one solidified crystalline structure, one amplified irradiated formed state, one piercing force before it was segregated. Now let's take all those particles before any mass particles were created, before there was any formless state created, before any un-manifest form was created, before a thought of a thought was created, before any physicality and before any segregated facet of any particle anywhere - just one solidified crystalline facet without any space around that crystalline form - and we will call that *Creator*. That is you. Creator, before there was any *splitting-off* [3] of a whole totality of a relationship as the self, with oneself, without segregation nor separation; simplistically, you without duality nor judgment of oneself.

Creation of the physical started when you as Creator decided amongst one's self, and upon one's self, to begin to expand upon one's self; when you began as a whole, to question, *I wonder what it would be like to expand upon myself, to feel what it was like to begin to express in a solidified, magnificent form, solidified form?* Expansiveness is who you are; complete particles of light, particles of gold, of no confinement, no solidification. There are no bounds, no barriers; hence, what so many share about unlimitedness. Unlimitedness is unlimitedness; but regardless, you as a formless Creator Particle said, "*Hey wouldn't it be brilliant to begin to express, to grow, to learn about myself through*

---

[3] Splitting-off; a split cell (we can also just call it another particle of the solidified crystalline facet) is playing with magnetization, no more different than playing with atomic and sub-atomic particles. When playing with de-magnetizing, you are playing with particles that are no longer connected with each other.

a manifest solidified form, to even create a form of such beautiful particles of animation in a solidified form to emanate so many facets of brilliance, so many different facets of uniquedness and to even learn about myself further?" Let's not forget, you as Creator, Creator as Creator, the facet that you are as Creator, is learning about itself, growing about itself, expanding on itself. That's the beauty here. Even your all-knowingness is growing about knowingness, even contemplating its own knowingness to know more about its knowingness. You as Creator are learning about yourself and even contemplating yourself about your own contemplations about yourself. There are no barriers, no bounds to exploring and expanding upon yourself well beyond spaciousness; you are even creating spaciousness within your own spaciousness and beyond spaciousness to a point where there are no bounds at all.

Now from here, so much more began to unfold, because you as Creator decided to split yourself off in the physical form. So here you are opening as Creator, expanding upon creation, within and throughout creation. You as Creator, you as this isness in the physical can command this and that so; and so it is, because now you are expanding a particle of yourself and there's really no end to what you can explore, because you are Creator expanding upon yourself through creation. There's just no end throughout creation to what you can, will and do expand upon and play with; so now you have creation and beyond to enjoy overtime. Now I say play and enjoy, because you're not going to take it seriously; you are just honoring that you are Creator, expanding upon creation. Now as you are Creator expanding upon creation, explore how much further you can, as Creator, evolve upon yourself; because let's not forget that you as Creator are growing, remembering and evolving. The whole point of why you're even playing here is to express, to explore, to wake up and to take off upon yourself as Creator in the physical.

Including your Creator level, there are other realms, or shall I say levels of you, that I'll call your *higher levels*, your *big guns*, your *entourage*. Your higher levels are you; higher vibratory levels, the beautiful tones, frequencies, the light-beingness, the realms in which you truly, thoroughly vibrate at; the tones the frequencies, the higher plains, the faster plains, the vibratory resonations in frequencies of megahertz in which you and your body truly vibrate, in which the cells vibrate, in which higher tones, the hues, the frequencies and sounds, and even the color facets you'll play with, which is total complete gold. They are also realms in which your manifest levels, your embodiment levels, your angelic, archangelic realms, your ascended hosts and your guidance realms also resonate in. It's the plains beyond the dimensional plains. It's also the dimensional plains all collapsing into one, which is also the translucentness of all the veils opening and unraveling all around you. It's where all the auric levels dissolve and transcend beyond the soul level and the akashic record realms, to where all of it is actually unveiled and peeled away and laid flat all around you, to where everything around you is total complete light, is total complete gold, is total complete wide-open-ness.

Your higher levels are your realms of light, your realms of divinity, your realms of total complete fruition, your realms of gold, your realms of enjoyment, your realms of exuberance as well, because from these realms of exuberance, enjoyment; we'll call them joy, we'll call them bliss, we'll call them love, we'll call them light-beingness; it's your natural state of divinity. Because in these states of natural divinity is also your natural state of omnipotence. It's your natural birthright to be in a total state of flourishment, exuberance, bliss, enjoyment, your love-state, your light-state. It's letting your whole outside world begin to work for you rather than you working for it. It's also your natural state of abundance as well; abundance of love, abundance of light-beingness, abundance of money. It's also letting your outside world totally, completely, thoroughly open up and flourish and be given to you.

You are unique in a body on this planet and your essence, your higher realms, your entourage are providing you with circumstances and opportunities to uniquely assist your highest and best good, to best complement you into running forth into everything faster than ever so that you can completely enjoy all of creation in your fullest of potential and much more. You then are literally dancing with the whole Universe throughout all the beautiful, priceless, orchestrated events of your divine unfoldment that are coming to life; diverse turns that have their own journeys within journeys for their own specific reason (beyond analytical reasoning) to come forth, to complement the whole of the rest of what is going on around you. Your higher realms are providing you one offer, then another offer and then another, to honor you, to celebrate you and to give to you, to sing with you and to dance with you and most importantly, to complement you in every way on every realm, in every facet of creation with continued openings and with facets that have not quite been opened throughout creation. These facets that have not quite been opened are anxiously awaiting your permission and arrival.

These particles, opportunities and circumstances that are being presented to you are not you and will never be you, which can drive you batty when you identify with them. It is how you dance with them that matters and how you let them work for you, rather than to identify with them and let them be you or about you. These particles, opportunities and circumstances are also sharing that this assistance is not about happiness, for when you are living as the pure consciousness, of and as your divine essence, there is not good nor bad; there just *Is,* and you are being steered right out of the density into your complete lightness and brilliance.

For as your higher levels are giving you opportunities, offers and gifts, why would you work so hard and listen to your lower levels of consciousness that say; "*I have to, must do, should do?*" Why would you listen to your lower levels, all the physical, mental, and emotional levels that have been commanding and demanding from the outside world that you have to do this, you have to do that, you must do this, you must do that, and you should and you ought to, on and on and so forth? All these rules and barriers have been handed to you, tossed upon you from the mental psyche, sub-psyche and emotional levels that have been, once again, handed to you from the mental bodies, from what a societal level has tossed to you, from genetic levels and from the family monads[4] as well. These layers have been forced upon you and handed upon you for eons and generations and are what the mental and emotional levels have called familiarity.

The body-principle has nothing to say about it because it's only been taking on all these colorful barriers, rules; we'll call it jargon, because it's all of these assumptions that have been made of how everything is supposed to work, everything that's been taught to work, from all of these carnal levels, which are all your lower levels. Remember; from your higher levels, from your heart level, your throat level, your pineal-pituitary gland and also from the human genome itself, that works so brilliantly, all the way from your DNA, your master-cell of consciousness, which is where your youth-and-vitality chromosomes exist, as well as the telomere, all the way through your crown chakra level vortex, which is also where everything is activating and activating, constantly regenerating itself as well, from your crown level chakra level vortex, right through the master-cell of consciousness, everything is quite naturally regenerating, rebuilding, and also playing with your gold realms of DNA and your Universal DNA, because your Universal state of DNA are constantly growing, regenerating, activating all the way through your whole physicality; rewriting itself in your image, rather than the image the body principle came with, rather than what has been embodied.

---

[4] Monad: The soul group/family that you were born into.

Genetics have nothing to do with you any longer, nor are you a part of a genetic pool any longer, because you are reclaiming you and your body.

So let's welcome forth your higher realms, your angelic, arch-angelic, ascended host realms and your guidance realms into your life-stream. Your higher realms are merging and marrying with you, clearing away, cleansing away, purifying away all the identificational realms, all barriers, all the - we'll call it metaphoric blockages, egoic structures - that have been implemented in place, locked into your lower levels, your physical, mental and emotional levels. It's all your higher plains that say; *"What are you doing here? Why are you taking things so serious here? Why are you getting so hijacked here? Why is all this colorful stuff all around you seemingly so important? Why is all this stuff around you totally, thoroughly taking and being given all this power and being made to be so overbearing? Why are all these overbearing layers and levels running over your life-stream, taking over your life-stream, hijacking you, taking you here, taking you there; when really, none of it at all has anything to do with you? And as it doesn't have anything to do with you why are you allowing it to become embedded? Why are you embodying it? Why are you even making it to be about you?"* says your angelic, archangelic, ascended-host realms, says you as Creator as well; *"Why is all this stuff around seemingly so important? And remember, it has nothing to do with you, has nothing to do with us,"* says your angelic, archangelic, ascended-host realms. *"Remember, you're here to remember who you are. Remember, you are here to sing and dance and flourish and let the outside world also accommodate and complement you and open up and flourish with you."*

Your higher levels have to do with everything constantly regenerating, rebuilding, re-amplifying, re-writing, re-opening, re-writing the encodements of consciousness through your physicality, because now you're reclaiming your physicality as your physicality, no longer the product of brother humanity or the family genomes, or even the family genetic streams. You are reclaiming your life-stream and your higher levels are bringing themselves right through the lower levels. Your lower levels being your solar plexus realm, your gender principle and your root-chakra level vortex. Now from all these lower levels, you have been taking on all of creation and the outside world, and working so much here when you need not do so any longer, because none of it has to do with you.

When you start to arise and welcome in your manifest levels, Creator levels, higher levels to take command, speak through you, steer you and journey you, even take command of the physicality, just say; *"Higher levels, take command of the liver, take command of the pancreas, take command of the lower levels; as a matter of fact higher levels, start transcending them, because I am ready and I want to know who I am. Bring it on; take command of the finances, take command of my soul, my life, my work, my wealth, my mind, my body, my world. I am done with carnality. I am done with survival. I am done playing with all of these conflicting, challenging levels, all of these different traits, all of these different dynamics, all of these different unfoldments, all of these different plains of consciousness that have nothing to do with me. Be gone with everything that has nothing to do with me."* Now you can let your life take on its own life because it has its own life. Even all the sequences of events have their own life. It all has its own unfoldments in which you can take part in, enjoy, grow and grow.

Letting your life take on its own life is not letting the mind level dictate how it's going to be done and when it's going to be done and letting the mind level begin to run you. When you let things take on their own life, you are letting them be a dance and letting it all come to life. A dance is more of a fluidity where everything takes on its own life and its own unique lives, in so many different directions, to complement you and the whole. A dance goes back and forth. You are going to move this way to the left and another whole bunch of unfoldments take place in the space that you moved from, which give the opportunity for both to emerge in a dance as your feet are metaphorically off the ground and being led to the right and left, again to the right and then the left; the opportunities, openings and mergings are created to complement and assist you, because there is no longer any repetition nor any necessity for comfort and there is truly no discomfort because you are in a Universal dance and seeing physical, tangible, divine results that of course, complement and add to your life exquisitely.

You are literally walking, dancing and flourishing right through the beautiful aeration and lightness of letting your *big guns* move forth and come through into your life-stream. You are letting the whole Universe open and carry your life-stream, nourishing your life-stream far beyond anything you could ever comprehend or imagine as an egoic or an emotional wanting. This is a life opening and heart-felt eye opening that moves you forth without a finite direction; a calling that allows direction to come forth and it is a direction that has no end and yet only continues to grow. This is truly called a relationship with your higher levels, your Creator levels, the whole Universe entirely.

This is who you are.

A True Loving Relationship of the Heart with Your Life-Stream, Your Beingness and the Whole Universe

A true loving relationship of the heart with your life-stream, your beingness and the whole Universe is an in-depth, passionate relationship that allows for the giving of your uniqued expression and at the same time, receiving from your expression. This is creating a cyclical dance of going out and coming in. The giving and receiving are one; one's heart opening and opening, where you are no longer only feeling from a lower level of creation, and no longer just feeling from a higher level of creation. It is coming from every facet, of every particle of the physical being, which is in a total open expression that is growing upon itself in every way. This is creation as creation was created to be. This is what you can call a true relationship of the heart - a total constant communion of love.

As you let you expose yourself to you, there is no polarity called *offense* or *defense*. There is light. There is true love. Love beyond unconditionalness. Love that is a constant love that needs no forgiveness. Love that even needs no figuring out or understanding. Love beyond knowingness; it is a constant. It is a constant fruition, a constant expandedness and growingness, expanding upon itself, pulling in, coming out, coming out and pulling in; breathing upon itself. It's a constant.

For the only dis-ease here, the only conflict, is the lack of love, or shall I say the lack of you. It is primality. It is a defense. It's also the angst of an offense or protectiveness; but yet, it's still the absence of you. It has nothing to do with a relationship, not even with oneself. It has to do with the absence of a relationship. It has everything do with the automated, automatic pilot of primality, carnivorousness; the carnivorousness that has nothing to do with eating meat, not eating meat, eating vegetables, not eating vegetables. It has nothing to do with the outside. It has everything to do with work and domination.

So now as you just let your love grow and expand upon itself; expand upon itself within every particle of your being, without any understanding, without even the attempts of understanding, why don't you just let it happen? Why don't you not even give so much credibility to a mental level of emotional habla, emotional deities, mental habla, mental levels that are attempting to try to hook-in, get involved, get engaged, to try to put things into certain places, certain formulae, certain formalities for its own survival, for its own clarity. Why don't you just put all that aside; because the mental level cannot even for one second understand love. It cannot even understand you. It can try. But why let it confine you? Why let it, even for one iota, attempt to hold you from you?

In this true relationship of the heart with your life-stream, you are dancing, playing, affecting, transcending and transpiring with what is in front of you, without reaction, without taking on events within and without the embodiment of you. Now you are truly assisting, amplifying and transcending all that is in your out-picturing world. Now as the world has nothing to do with you, you have it made. Now that you are affecting things outside of you and dancing with everything exponentially, you have it made.

If opportunities and circumstances start to become about you, or a part of you, that is when you can start to let them drive yourself batty. It starts to shut you down and polarize you to the point that you are changing all the Universal dynamics. You are getting wrapped up into the polarized dynamics that start to become a part of you and about a you; and you have just created a lot of work for oneself that need not be work. You have created a life of defense rather than fluidity. As you begin to let others affect you, due to a false sense of a mental idea of a self, and begin to take on these ideas such as a false sense of responsibility, a false sense of compassion, a false sense of feeling good about oneself or not, you are creating a life of carnality and primality.

One of the biggest perceptions is that within your life-stream you are going to have highs and lows, etc. As you are bypassing all the mental jargon, because none of that is accurate, as you do not contemplate your relationships and simply run with them, as you are letting the rest of you - beyond the mind - come forth to fully and completely honor you, letting the love, the enjoyment, the embodiment and embracement of you happen, letting dear brothers into your life-stream while at the same time keeping the periodic conflicts of dear brothers outside of you, as you are in total and complete enjoyment with all of it and no longer creating judgments[5] on what has to be and what cannot be, you are flowing without all the identificational states of *it should be, it must be, what something is not,* or *what is missing, etc.*; you are no longer going into a withdrawal state, nor a conflicted state, nor a rigid state, nor a confined state. How about you let everything come into alignment for you, to complement you and to honor you? Just give the opportunities and events the go-ahead; *There it is. Let's go. There it is and bring it on. There it is and let it present. There it is and I am ready. Lets go.*

So let's give the go-ahead and let your angelic, arch-angelic, ascended host realms, your guidance realms into your life-stream, letting them take care of all of the calamities, the conflicted states, the identified embodied behavioral mannerisms; letting the behavioral mannerisms, conflicts, etc., all die off so you are no longer confined by one certain state or another, no longer living in a protectiveness, nor affected by emotional deities[6], and no longer living in a protective state of the mental level, no longer living in a protective state of what can be and cannot be, has to be,

---

[5] Appendix B: Judgment - Empathy and Sympathy
[6] A deity is a presence outside of yourself, deemed to be made into a reality. Deities are live levels of consciousness around you from the outside.

etc. You are no longer living in a protective state of *I have to be strong,* and automatically pushing everything else away. You are playing with the angelic, arch-angelic, ascended host realms and beyond. Let's remember that these are priceless dear brothers - a priceless entourage - and yet they are not you and you are not them. They are your entourage and your family. There is so much more to you than the mental levels perceive, so much more available for you. You can venture so much further than your mind could ever contemplate or imagine. Let's let a relationship with oneself arise, to relate and interrelate, letting all particles mesh and meld together without a personality so that you can arise as a total pristine facet of clarity and beauty throughout the whole Universe.

Why is there so much busyness going on within you about other dear brothers' mental levels running this way and that way? They are doing their utmost to find their way back to their heart. From their heart they are looking for their pathway home while on the planet; the heart being the state of one with all that is, the heart being a state of a communion of oneself with Creator. Please, if you choose, welcome your entourage into your life-stream and let them take care of removing the conflicts, debris, beliefs, etc., that are preventing you from experiencing you.

As you are watching all the beautiful, priceless, dear brothers run in countless directions, some are wanting to bring you in their directions, some wanting you to support their behavioral mannerisms, some wanting to take you over and have you be submissive. All of that is fine as you are saying to yourself; "*Higher levels take command, steer me, journey me. I am awake. Now keep me awake. I am not going to run away from it. I am going to walk one step after another right through it. Higher levels take command. Let it unfold."*

At this point, let's not evaluate what is going on with yourself, and the *how did I attract this, etc.* What you are playing with is not going within; you are going without, right into the outside world. You're no longer looking for deep dark hidden secrets, nor any conflictedness. You are only seeing it for what it is; all of these Creators Incarnate, all of these facets of divinity, walking around doing whatever they are doing; and let's remember, you are not any of these dear brothers' conflicts. That is not where you are playing. You are just walking through it. As you are walking through with these dear brothers, let's continue to show up, once again, watching what is happening outside of you and around you.

As you are watching what is happening, not observing, literally watching, while still doing your part and walking your walk overtime, let's honor that you are not a part of the whole here. You are an instrument within it. *I am awake. Now keep me awake. Keep me clear. I am a clear facet of divinity in a body on a planet.* Let's not stand for your truth, nor give away your truth. Let's not even have a truth. Let's just watch what is happening. Let's not let yourself mentally, emotionally, nor physically, have anything to hold onto here. Let's just let everything that is running its course around you, run its course around you. Let's just be the clear and perfected facet of divinity that you are. You are in it and not of it. You are in it to transcend it and let it transcend around you.

Now, as you are not joining one camp or another, let's watch the barbed wire between the camps begin to break down as well. Remember the barbed wire cannot be there unless you are going to take one side or another, unless you are going to be a part of the dominators or the dominated. As you watch the chasm between these camps, how much of it is lighting on fire? Watch all the dissolvement happening. Watch all the literal and physical changes happening around, within your own presence. Let's just continue to run forth and watch how unscathed you are via not picking a side. Picking a side is a total and complete angst of a relationship with who you are. It is a total and complete breakdown of a segregated facet of you and it becomes one facet of you challenging another. Choosing between camps becomes a never-ending battle until you decide there is no choice to choose and there is everything to play with here. You are there as a conduit and a facilitator, not supporting one cause or another.

As you show up and continue to watch everything happening around you, watch how you show up without any agenda nor any perceptional judgments, because why have an agenda when it does not have anything to do with oneself? It is what it is. No more and no less. It is what it is; and now it is what you do with it, how you play with it and where you let it go. *All right Creator levels, manifest levels, Universe* - it matters not what you call it, it is still you - *take charge. I am awake now keep me awake. Speak through me, steer me and journey me. I am a clear and pure channel for divinity and love. Speak nothing but exquisite love, wholeness and divinity from these lips.*

There's not one dear brother on the planet that is a victim. Either you are going to show up or not. You may attempt to be a victim or even victimized; yet there is no dear brother on this planet without opportunities and there are many who find a reason not to show up and many perceptional, justifiable conditions why you did not show up. You will step up when you are ready. Opportunities will keep presenting and being offered for you, from love and as a priceless gift to honor you and to complement you, and it is up to you; how low you want to go before you start taking steps towards the opportunities that present, is up to you. No matter when you decide to step through them, you are loved, adored, honored and assisted always.

If sequences of events start to become about you, or a part of you, that is when you will begin to drive yourself batty again. You are shutting yourself down and polarizing yourself to the point you are changing all the Universal dynamics. You are getting wrapped up into polarized dynamics that are becoming a part of you and about a perceived you; and you have just created a lot of work for oneself that need not be work. You have created a life of defense rather than fluidity. You are creating a life of carnality and primality as you welcome others to affect every particle of your being due to a false sense of responsibility, a false sense of compassion, a false sense of feeling good about yourself, or not feeling good about yourself. Now you may want to examine who is running yourself and life-stream; other dear brothers, yourself, or neither; also asking yourself, "*Wow, why have I let my mind/ego take over so powerfully? What are the barriers that are trying to be protected?*"

If you find yourself caught up in your mind, just say to yourself, "*Congratulations, you have done it again*"; and then the real congratulations presents as you are watching your mind and seeing it for what it is. Wow, isn't that easy? So, when you catch yourself contemplating and analyzing your relationship with your mind, about how your relationship is, how it should work and how it should be, now you can stop and get silent, still, reconnect with you essence, ask yourself, "*What am I going to do about this?*" and let present what actions to take or not to take to be the love that you are no matter what the circumstances are. For some, being one with your essence may be difficult at first, but do it anyway. At first, use any and all tools you have learned until it becomes natural, because it is natural. It is you. Whatever stage of consciousness you are at, let the action present and go with it, because when there is no right and wrong it does not matter what is on the other side of your actions.

If you have to do this 100 times a day at first, that is great, because the next day you may only need to do it 90 times, the next week 50 times, the next month 20 times, the next year 5 times, etc. Once you are watching your mind and your thoughts, you are not in your mind. Once you watch the angst, the emotion, you are not in your mind. Now it comes to being able to flourish and emanate, letting the rest just simplistically dissolve without all of this work that need not take any work at all, and you can just simply have all sorts of enjoyment and exquisite love, romance and passionate relationships all around you.

Isn't it amazing when you don't have to be in charge? Wow, talk about a brilliant, priceless life-stream that is filled with nothing but total complete clarity, light-beingness, Creator Consciousness and the beautiful gift of love all around you; not trying to have to sort through, filter through, not trying to find the love in the darkness, so forth and so forth; not even trying to find the light in the darkness, because isn't it amazing where there is no darkness there is no density? Isn't it brilliant where you can just have a blast; a very integrated, embodied blast exponentially, without having to filter, sort, become safe or in a false sense of comfortability from all these colorful comfort zones of what the magazines or media say, or what the sitcoms say, what brother humanity says, what all the greeting cards say and so forth?

What happens when love comes to you through a complete, brilliant, priceless stream of sequenced events, without interruptions, without all of these colorful filters in place? There's you. There's emanation. There's love. Isn't it amazing when we just let love in; no past, no present, no future, not even a now, but beautiful particles of light-beingness eminently expanding upon itself; and you, as Creator Incarnate, the love that is being presented for you, around you, through you and as you, completely being offered to you with no identifications that it has to be *this, that,* and *I have to protect my self,* whatever self is here.

Because self is quite colorful; it's a self of barriers. It's a self that only begins to become dualistic and polarized, segregated, separated; but where's the all encompassness? Where is the unanimous, infinite love without bounds that knows no bounds to a singularity of a confined self? Isn't it odd where there are all these rules that you have to get up, put on your costumes, go to work, do this, do that, have the approval, give the approval, be understood, so forth and so forth, to let things start to run forth and move? Don't you find that a little bit peculiar? You have to wear this costume, wear that costume, get the fingernails painted, putting on makeup this way and that way to maybe be tantalizing, appetizing, attractive to another; so maybe, maybe, maybe they will love you. What does that have anything to do with love or you?

So let's go get your nails painted, your face painted and all that fun stuff if you enjoy it, to only accent your beauty, to accent your brilliance; but let's not forget about you within it. It's still the love that's being called for, being yearned for to the heart of another, no longer from a need, no longer from a good enough, worthiness and all the mental habla; love is love is love, and then letting the love carry you, letting your higher levels, your Creator levels, your manifest levels, your angelic levels the ascended host realms, your guidance realms, your family, your entourage, bring forth to you the whole buffet of divinitization, the whole buffet of purification, the whole buffet of the beauty of your natural birthright, the beauty of the total love that you've been giving the go-ahead for and asking for.

Well, can't you just let it start to happen? Let love light up love. Letting your heart level open and your heart level open the hearts of others. But yet, can you let your *big guns*, your Creator levels, manifest levels, your higher levels, the whole Universe entirely that is so unanimous, has no bounds, no barriers, give to you without the debris from all of the past scenarios? Can you just let your *big guns* take command and let the love flow, because now you're playing with the divine relationship of the heart? Now you're playing with the true divine relationship that's been awaiting you, that has been opening and that you've been yearning for anyway, for the enjoyment, the prosperity of love, expanding upon love without any colorful barriers there. So once again, even though you're asking, *"Can I?"* it really comes down to, *Will you?* Because *will you, is will you. Love is love is love. Lightness is lightness is lightness*; you honoring you, no if, ands or buts about it. Are you willing to let yourself be the love that you are?

From here, let's just let it arise. *It, being you. It, being your presence. It, being the light that you have always been, the light-beingness that you have always been, the particles of consciousness that you have always been and you always will be.*

A true loving relationship of the heart within your life-stream is a true relationship with all that is, and going into the true embodiment of the Universe through the physical – a relationship of totality. This is a state where love is love is love, and you are letting creation happen around you. This is a state where you know what matters for you, to you, because when a sequence or an event, a *this thing* or *that thing* happens, you feel brilliant, exquisite, vibrant, expressive, lively, enriched; which all equals love and openness.

A True Loving Relationship of the Heart with Another

A true loving relationship of the heart, a marriage of the heart with another, is coming from an open-heartedness and a welcoming and letting a relationship of the heart with another come forward from a state of *I am healthy, whole and complete in every way* and *show me what's next.* You are coming from a fully integrated state of letting another dear brother present for you within your life-stream, from a total and complete communion, from a total and complete relatedness, to where there are no barriers; there is no seeking, there is no *I have everything but...*, and there is no part of yourself missing or lacking. There is not a lack of total fluidity within your life-stream. There is harmoniousness, unconditional love, openness, equality, etc., and there is an openness for an arisement of a total and complete, complementary communion of the heart with another where you are adding to each other's life-streams.

In this openness, the other dear one arises and you now have two hearts becoming one with three separate journeys; your journey, their journey and your journey together. These journeys are complementing each other without any holding back, rules and barriers; your life-streams begin to become one, and here there is no work to be done, there is no one to take care of, or be taken care of by another, there are no issues to process and no one is broken; there is total enjoyment as you walk together side-by-side. This enjoyment is specifically and eminently there for you to come into each other's life-streams; for you give unto one another, which is also giving unto your life-stream and your outside world together, to be only that of a nurturing quality, to add upon the enjoyment of the exquisiteness of creation. You no longer are within a state of *I have this identity* and *you have that identity, I have this structure to break down* and *you have that structure to break down and process, etc.* It is a state of total and complete enjoyment of creation to be given to, and to open upon itself without any barriers, without any scores to be taken, nor rules required. It is a state of being offered unto and given unto Universally as the beautiful, Universal, harmonious, Creator Incarnate that you are, able to enjoy every facet of creation, from the enjoyment of abundance, to the enjoyment of endeavors together that are arising vibratorally. It is also arising within the wide openness for one another, to one another and exponentially to the outside world, stepping into another whole world together dimensionally, physically and full-heartedly, which is adding unto creation and opening up upon itself to be expressed, explored, enjoyed and run through.

This state is the true divine normality of what a relationship was created to be. It is no longer about the divine feminine, or divine masculine, as none of that matters any longer. It is no longer about patterns, nor of who does what when and how to fit into structures, upon structures, to attempt to do one thing or another. How many things are growing upon themselves is the only thing that Universally matters; it is there to play with, and the openness to play with whatever else presents to play with. There is no end, only a divine beginning.

When two presences come together there is nothing other than pure and complete emanation without work; there is love, honorability and integrity. There are no rulebooks here, nor work necessary. Your heart and *big guns* are taking over. You are letting the relationship as the deity, the light-beingness, the beautiful gift, the joy and the love that it is, take on its own life and become its own life. As it is taking on its own life, it is growing upon itself, without all the primal, carnal levels of rules that are based in fear about protecting and nurturing something that need not be protected, nor nurtured, because it has a life of its own. For example, let's say there is a certain opportunity, a dinner date with you, your partner and both of your parents. You both are going to jump right into it together, side-by-side, as one heart. It's not about your partner's monad, nor your monad. It is about the other dear brothers in front of you, to whom you are presenting together, as one heart exponentially, through the dinner date and so much more. It is about brother humanity outside of you both; you are dancing with them together. The other dear brothers are around you and you are representing one love and one Universe, through all the ones around you, no longer whom is whom and who plays which way. It is about your one love emanating through the other dear brothers around you.

What is love, beyond actions, words and deeds? What is love, beyond toys and gifts, abundances? What is love, beyond behavioral mannerisms? As you're exploring the love of another, or shall I say letting it unfold and letting it come forth, how much is your body principle, right now, un-anchoring and unhooking as the vibratory principles of it (the speed in which the cells are moving) are metamorphosizing, changing, re-amplifying and re-writing in your image; the image beyond carnality, the image of a beautiful priceless genome, called a beautiful spark, a beautiful facet of light-beingness and Creator Incarnate; the beautiful pure consciousness, pure particles of one pure thought of going into the primality of thought; the primality before the primal instinct or separation was even created that says; *"I am lovable. I am love. What am I afraid of? Why would I push away an intimate, loving, priceless relationship with myself for another? Why would I survive or strive? What am I working so hard for to keep another away, or to keep another with me? Why is there any work here at all? What has this all been about?"*

Why has a relationship even begun to start to become work? Relationships don't take work; defense does, primality most definitely does, the winning, the losing does, the *who's going to have the control, the domination, the responsibility for the whole, taking care of the whole,* putting it into the body principle and so forth, that's a lot of work. But yet, what does that have to do with love? Where did that even come from besides carnality, survival and the carnality of superseding another to gain momentum within your own life-stream, to gain the power; the power of domination that's collapsing anyway and truly equals aloneness and nothingness.

Your mind cannot comprehend all the facets of divinity and will just attempt to make something out of nothingness. Within the new relationships that are presented, just give them the go-ahead; *there it is, let's go.* So much has been taken in by dear ones, using colorful definitions of why this occurred and who I am etc., based on other dear brothers' behaviors, even though it doesn't have anything to do with oneself. Let's please forget about evaluating what everything looks like, as nothing presents for the sake of presenting. Let's not make it more than it is. It's presenting to complement you.

Let's please forget about being with people with whom you resonate, or with whom you have similar interests. As you no longer are seeking common resonances you can now go forward and enjoy your life overtime, no matter what the circumstances, because you don't have any barriers nor blockages to remove, and no mountains to climb to be with dear ones in order to resonate with them. You can simply just let the love in; *Let*, being the key word here. Let yourself be divinely, brilliantly and omnipotently okay with yourself and okay with the outside world; no longer looking for a battle, no longer looking for structure and no longer looking for something to take over, or be taken over by, just for a validation of a false sense of an egoic structure that is giving a false sense of value upon yourself, so that you can give yourself a false sense of value rather than being who you are. How can you not resonate with anyone? You are Creator Incarnate here. Would you suppose your Creator Consciousness would be biased to one dear brother to another? Of course not. It sees nothing but love. It sees dear brothers that are dancing back and forth and yes, some dear brothers having conflicts all over the place; and all is well. But wouldn't you also suppose, maybe, these dear ones are looking to do their utmost to run beyond it, to rise to love beyond the egoic conflicts? But yet, why would you shut yourself down, polarize yourself, your heart, your relationships of the heart, your brilliant, divine divinity, just because the dear brother before you is running through a lot of mental, emotional debris?

Another false sense is a dear one having a dating resume that says, *"In order for another dear brother to come into my life-stream, they must first pass through the metaphoric eye of the needle."* For example, the other dear brother has to pass through and supersede right through all these rules, to reach a state where the dear one will be in a certain stature to be allowed to come into my life-stream; and guess what, they are never going to be able to arise to the challenge, because the rules and challenges are too high, too rigid and they are obstacles that are not achievable. They are obstacles that have been locked into place from all of the angst and rigidity that has occurred throughout your life-stream. These rigidities have created a false sense of emotions, a false sense of worthiness, a false sense of primal survival, etc. These states have nothing to do with your real self. These states can end once you decide; *I'm taking everyone off trial. I'm even taking myself off trial. I am just going to let myself be loved. I'm also going to begin to explore what love really is.*

Why don't you just let love, for a moment, continue to grow and grow and if you're going to have a focal point, how about your focal point just be; *I wonder how much I can have a blast with everyone on this planetary matrix? I wonder how I can have a blast with all of these brilliant, priceless diversities that have been presenting around me? I wonder how much I can just totally, thoroughly enjoy all the brilliant diversities of facets that have come into my life-stream and that are within my life-stream? I wonder how much I can just really, thoroughly enjoy having a blast and sing and dance, without even trying to understand?* So let's not give it that much credibility. Let's just enjoy the dear ones around us when you can just be and enjoy the emanation, the vibrancy and brightness that you are with all concerned. Why don't we just call love your natural state; a state of brilliance, a state of beauty, and of course your natural birthright, because it simply just is.

So as you toss all the mental jargon into the ethers and all the emotional states into the ethers, what and whom cannot you not have a blast with? It's not as though you're taking dear brothers' issues to make them your own. It's not as though anyone is broken, because no one is broken. Dear ones are just at different places; and all is well. But why would you ever polarize yourself with these colorful filters, barriers, to let yourself be so colorfully, dynamically polarized and withdrawn from letting the beloved of your heart present themselves? Love is love is love; everywhere, within all realms, humanity, angelic, archangelic, ascended hosts, guidance realms, etc. Why would you close yourself down and become afraid of humanity, but be wide open to your angelic presences? Why would you welcome in your *big guns* to start to let everything present around you, but then start to push areas away when you're also being steered and journeyed right to a beautiful beloved to come into your life-stream, without any barriers, without any conflicts, but yet to sing and dance and flourish overtime; no better, no less, no good, no bad, no more than, no less than and all this colorful stuff.

Now as you look at these dear hearts, why don't you also watch all of these beautiful dear ones running around, right where they're unfolding within their own journeys. Why don't you also, simplistically, be the huge, brilliant, divine, conduit here. Why don't you be wide open to let all of these priceless journeys come in around you from so many directions; some being moved out, some being moved in, the job dynamics being scattered, changed around, metamorphosized, re-organized, to most simply and beautifully let dear brothers come into your life-stream from everything you've been giving the go-ahead to and for, from a total complete open-heartness, openness, divinity and brilliance and be able to dance with all that is.

So right now, as your vibratory levels are speeding up, amplifying exponentially, why don't you decide to have no defense. Why don't you also decide to search for nothing. Why don't you also decide, right here and now, not to look for anything and let everything start to expose itself; for you see, if you let it expose itself, there is nothing here to be without. As you are now giving the go-ahead to opportunities and relationships without all of the evaluations, now you are at an ending point and are willing to step up when dear ones present. *Bring on the divine relationship of my heart and let's have a blast.*

In a relationship of the heart with another, the most important facet within the relationship is the underlying core, the underlying current, the underlying love and passion of the hearts coming together full force; and the intellectual levels, the camaraderie levels and every level of creation comes together, individually, uniquedly and then together. In a relationship of the heart with another there is so much more love emanating from both parties because of everything you are playing with together, and exponentially emanating together; and there is a whole new life-stream to be explored.

Excellent Questions Asked by Many Dear Ones

"What About Other Types of Relationships...

I have heard of other types of relationships in addition to a Relationship of the Heart, such as *Divine Complements, Twin Flames, Twin Souls and Relationships from Zero Karma.* What are they about?"

Divine Complements:

When a relationship becomes a power game it can be categorized as a *Divine Complement*, not a relationship of the heart. Your Divine Complement is a relationship where you are playing with emotional debris and you are going to throw it back and forth to each other, to push each other further. This is totally different from a relationship/marriage of the heart. A marriage/relationship of the heart is a total, complete, priceless communion, even when dear brothers withdraw temporarily, but yet continually share, *all is well and I love you no matter what.*

Within a Divine Complementary state of relationship, many times dear brothers play, *I am totally playing in love, I am totally playing in conflict*, and back and forth, and back and forth between these states. This is where the mind gets so intertwined and involved that you start to push away from transcending into the heart level completely. Then you start bringing in your incarnational journeys and of course you have had incarnational journeys, that's why you have the calling to be together and the familiarity about each other. When the head gets involved in the relationship and says; *"Now I know what I want and I am not going to settle, so you have to be what I want you to be, you have to be my dream come true checklist of qualities in order for me to enjoy and be happy"*, now you have another power game rather than the love unfolding and coming to life. The dear ones are not being brought into your life-stream for you to have battles with them. They are put into your life-stream to run forth with them, to celebrate and to enjoy and to express your divinitization with, no longer attempting to fix each other. You're not broken.

For some, you may wonder if the relationship level of Divine Complements can transition into a Relationship of the Heart very easily. Yes. Yes, when two hearts come together as one there is no turning back. When you are playing in a Divine Complement state, two dear brothers have come together side-by-side and it is an opportunity to come together and sing and dance overtime. The dear brothers still have emotional debris, yet if they let their heart levels come together, nothing else matters. It's a done deal, debris and all. You have two hearts walking together side-by-side as one heart, throughout all of humanity and the Universe. You are playing with and affecting all of brother humanity, the planet, the Universe and all that is, as well as letting the rest of your outside world open, metamorphosize all around you and so much more.

Twin Flames:

Twin Flames are a state of, *you are my feminine and I am your masculine*. Here you are playing with polarized states and split-soul states based in karma.

Twin Souls:

Twin Souls are two souls that have been split off and are emanating through two different genders and body principles to come together as one. They are two different journeyers, split off, that can come together to complement as a whole once again, eye to eye, heart to heart, to attempt to create a whole again through each other, and then look exponentially into the outside world and get to blaze right through and enjoy. Twin Souls were based in karma, which has now dissolved, although there are still dear brothers in a body on a planet acting out the karma they came in with.

Relationships from the Zero-Point Karma:

This is a whole additional journey. For people being born without karma, there is a complete marriage of the heart, DNA, the cellular vibratory levels, cellular inter-melding and inter-melding levels, an instant radiance that they begin to come together with emotional states being totally deflected and removed. They are coming together instantaneously with an intertwinement and inter-melding taking place, not to lose oneself within another, but to step into oneself with the other. They complement each other and spark off each other's DNA. Such is the case with Indigos - Double Indigos - Indigos having Indigos. Their relationship level is an inter-plane melding. They are filling the gap and breaking down the barriers of all the gaps; the karmic gaps that created Twin Souls and Twin Flames.

> *"Are relationships a job for doing...*
>
> *I have a lot of single friends seeking their relationship of their heart. They are dating people who they resonate with. They are finding that they are activating their partner in certain ways, kind of shaking the leaves of their branches, and then the relationship ends. Someone new comes along and will fall away, again and again. Why does this continue to happen?"*

Some feminine structures and some masculine structures are interpreting these intimate relationships as their job on the planet to assist dear ones to wake up without trying and not to settle, as if there is a job to do for the dear ones presenting, rather than to celebrate the priceless love and omnipotence that these dear ones, as well as the Universe, are bringing to you; and that is why they are not finding the relationship of the heart they are seeking. The next part is why would you seek, rather than let oneself find and be given to, for as you let yourself be given to, without expectations and barriers, you will be quite amazed at the beauty that is given to you.

Let's forget about work to be done on the planet. You are absolutely activating dear ones, pushing them forward and nudging them forward into their own journeys. The issue here is looking for someone with whom you resonate. Your mind is going to find dear ones that you intellectually resonate with and you will be with them for a short period of time until the intellectual relationship becomes dull. You will be bored and uninterested with their intellect, not out of a lack of love, or a lack of resonance. The reason is that the head level, the mind, is evaluating the resonance rather than you experiencing the utmost amplification, exuberance and vibrancy with your heart soaring like you always dreamed and have known it could be.

It's easy to pick a partner from the head/mind, where you resonate and enjoy the X, Y & Z of another dear one and then notice the A, B & C that you don't care for as much. Now your mind and emotions have a contemplation of what you think you are asking for and what you are not asking for. The reason these relationships are not lasting is because the dear ones are looking for someone using their mind and emotions, which has a resume of likes and dislikes, rather than going about your day and letting the dear one present that *you are infinite love* and can express infinite love and passion with and for; that love keeps arising and arising and coming to life more than ever now that you are with them and the expression of love and emanation continues to take on its own life, etc. Please start to just let the relationship with another take on its own life rather than seeking a relationship, rather than analyzing why your relationships are not lasting, why it is taking so long to find your relationship of the heart and all the other mental conflicts the mind can conjure up about your journey and relationships. The mind blames you and others for its discrepancies, rather than you flourishing and enjoying.

The dating/mating game becomes so colorful and the belief that you have so much work to do on this planet becomes so conflicting and so colorful. What work do you have to do on the planet? There is nothing you have to do on this planet. Once your head level becomes involved in your journey and expression, you can become part of a tidal wave of thoughts and conflicts. How much fun is it to become a part of the tidal wave? It becomes very dramatic and it does not become very exuberant. What happens when you don't have a job to do on this planet? You can just express, enjoy, lighten-up and let your higher levels, Creator levels, the whole Universe into your life to offer you a direction that gives you so much and now you are going with whatever presents around you, and in any and all places you are called to be in, without anything you have to do, without having to be an instrument or a conduit for others, nor having to assist anyone. Now you can fully be an instrument, a conduit of assistance more than ever, without any colorful, excess pressure or angst, constantly bringing it on.

What happens when you don't need a relationship and you let the relationship find you? You are playing with the receptiveness of love, honorability and communion. It doesn't matter if it is friendships, an intimate love of the heart, a business relationships, or if it is with your offspring. You are now being in your natural state of a complete engagement within being in a body on a planet, running into the outside world without any rigidity, nor holding oneself back, nor being held back by anyone or anything. You are letting yourself come forth fully and completely accessible to all of you, no longer one uniqued, sole-proprietorship journeyer alone, nor isolated, but yet wide awake and expressed, available, unaffectable as light, love, and never affected by density; but you are running forth and so is your world. You are letting your life-stream and all the other beautiful priceless dear brothers come forth to honor you, to sing with you, to dance with you and to complement you. As you are letting these dear brothers and different dynamics come forth to further complement your life-stream, all their issues, personal conflicts, misunderstandings, disgruntled natures, etc., that are dying out, you are not putting them to the sideline. You are addressing them as a priority for oneself to be in it, and not of it, to walk through it and not be withdrawn from it.

When you are one with your essence you are in a place of fluidity and your mind doesn't even check in to analyze opportunities and decisions. The clarity and the answers present fluidly and you go with them. Perhaps someone is yelling at you, that you should do this or you should have done that. From your state of fluidity, an honoring of all dear brothers, you can move things into a different direction, back into love and playfulness. You transcend it and open it up. There is always an option of how to respond. Are you going to be smaller and give your love and power away? Or, are you going to be the love that you are?

What if you said; *"Your yelling and comments don't resonate with me. You are attacking me and I am not willing to accept that behavior. This is your issue not mine."* What do you suppose would happen here? Would two parties become stagnated, lock horns and now be in a battle? Would there be egoic structure? Or, what if you said, *"Dear one, I love you dearly and how about we speak about this when we are less emotional so we can give this important topic the attention it requires and resolve it with clarity."*

"What about being Neutral in Relationships?"

Neutrality is a stepping-stone along your journey; and keep in mind, if you are neutral, *and I do mean only neutral*, you are now letting other dear ones run your life-stream rather than the whole Universe running your life-stream. What's running you is all of the outside input and information from other dear brother's perceptions of you, their idea of you, their perception of you via their creation levels of you, and at times, their certain wantings from you; agendas of how you fit into their life-streams, for their personal agendas for you and of you, for their survival. Make no mistake; it is not as though it is personal or conscious. It is not as though they do not love; but it is for survival or a false self, a mental level and emotional level that is doing its best to function, to strive, to survive, to matter. It is not about you. It is truly about the carnality of the functionability of the survival of an egoic structure, attempting to have a say within the life-stream that is in front of you.

If you are totally neutral, this is letting your life happen by chance, rather than being in a relationship with everything and everyone and letting it all transcend and ascend physically[7], Universally and pragmatically to complement you and all of creation. When you are in a relationship with everything and everyone, this is a state where you know what matters for you, to you, because you feel expansive, exquisite and enriched which equals love and openness, which is you.

"What about being Present in a Relationship?"

Being present takes a whole lot of work and you are going to go into overwhelm to be present with a dear one. You are going to do a whole lot of work to be present with a dear one and not become dyslexic and overwhelmed, and begin to embrace their personal conflicts, struggles, etc. You are going to attempt to be interested in the other dear one's issues and fix them. You are going to attempt to feel like what they are

---

[7] Transcend and ascend physically; by example, a dear brother who stepped up to a totally debilitated physicality and into playing two tennis matches in the same day, letting his body show him how its happy to provide a vibrant vehicle for him to enjoy.

saying matters to you, even when a whole lot of what is being said is nothingness and egoic chitchat, etc. The more you are attempting to be present with other dear brothers, the more you are attempting to be disengaged from the outside world and to be with them, you are shutting down your heightened awareness of everything else that is going on outside of you and within you. As you are doing your utmost to be present with them, and turning everything else off, *build-up* occurs, that continues to grow and is what you call being jolted, confined, pushed, challenged, the disciple of a little-self, etc., until you are no longer present. You begin to become in a beautiful fight with oneself; a struggle begins to occur out of complete nothingness. But wait a second, you are doing what is upright and justified and you are trying to be present with the dear one. Why is it not working? It is not working because the other dear one feels it as well, and it is not natural or fluid, and the love begins to metamorphosize into conflicts of the emotional deities.

How about you be *your presence*? In this state you see the presence, the gift of the other dear one. When you look at the beautiful presence of the dear one, you are not being pulled and fighting with one's self mentally, emotionally, or otherwise. You are able to enjoy the gift of a dear one, the brilliance of the dear one and the joy of dancing with the dear one from where they are coming from and where they are; because now, you don't have the work involved. Now you have fruition involved. When you are in your presence, you don't have all these analytical conflicts, nor observations building up as you attempt to be present and perceptually resonate with the other dear one, even in the areas where you don't perceptually resonate with dear ones.

When you are trying to be present, you'll notice that you have this build-up growing and growing, from the outside through the inside, from the inside through the outside of you. You also have a beautiful conflict growing while trying to be present. What you are really playing with is called confinement and stagnation as you are holding one's self back in the name of being present, in the name of peace, or at least the attempts of peace, attempts of catering and the attempts of honoring another dear brother. You can even call it the attempts of letting a dear brother know they matter. The other dear brother feels so important and initially you might as well, until you start to feel the stagnation and confinement of you and your true essence, then you have the battle of the mind and the heart. Now the conflicts are arising within you as you are playing with the dear one, who of course does matter, because they are in a body on the planet. Now you have to give, give, give and do, do, do more because now you are not playing with the heart level; you are playing with the mind level and a flagellation of an egoic arrogance that is getting nowhere really quick. For as you are creating, offering and feeding the other dear brother, in a way that has zero to do with love, zero to do with the intimacy of the heart and has zero to do with yourself, it has everything to do with a large rulebook of being thoughtful. It is a being present thoughtfulness that grows a lot of egoic expectations that go into a shutting down and withdrawing really quick, and into a lot of questioning and conflicts within oneself and even beginning to doubt oneself.

So let's look at the other side where you are being your presence. You now have two presences together where you are not going to ignore, bypass nor shut down a dear one, and you are going to run forth with them side-by-side. You are welcoming them forth to complement side-by-side; you are welcoming them to be thoroughly, completely and entirely enjoyed as you walk with them side-by-side as you are both flourishing.

Presences are always fluidly moving, dancing, being and becoming without work. Relationships don't take work. All of their requirements come divinely and naturally, in honesty, integrity and love. It is only when the mind makes it so complicated that you forget about your natural flow and divinity. When you let the mind/ego get involved, it creates complicatedness and more complicatedness. To feel this complicatedness, instead of *trying to be present*, why don't you just change that phrase and replace it with *trying to be stagnant and confining oneself,* and see it for what it is; a huge job to do that does not get you to the place that you already know is available for you – to be one with yourself. As you start to play with you, your presence, your brilliance and your beauty, you are starting to play with love, fruition, fluidity, movement, amplification, creation, openness, emanation and divine enjoyment – your complete birthright.

"How do we Overcome Issues...

How do we overcome relationship issues, seeing each other as the divine, while honoring ourselves?"

First and foremost when it comes to relationships, when you are connecting with another, even when they're having struggles, let's honor where they're coming from. Even when you're listening to what they're sharing, what they're saying, whether it be mental, analytical, emotional, egoic; even when it's being perceived from their heart, and you know full well it's not from their heart, you know very well it's from a mental, emotional egoic-structure, it's also a spewing out and even at times temper tantrums, blame games, what ever, however; let's just take our consciousness, for a moment, through your own heart level. Let's bring our presence right there. Let's let the spewing light up more than ever in a total state of neutrality, to start to feel even the particles moving in the palms of your hands, out your feet. But right here, let's just let the spewing continue from the beautiful, priceless dear brother before us. Let's just let the spewing go and go, letting it go wherever it wants to go; and now, without even saying a word let's take our consciousness and look right through their beautiful heart of who they truly are.

Let's let the spewing continue. The only thing I ask is that you not have any defense. Let's just all totally agree that they're right. Can you just let them all be right? So let's just totally let everyone be right. Let's look right through their heart level watching the beautiful, gold iridescence right there, regardless of all the spewing, all the struggles, all the pains. Let's not try to make it something that it is. Let's not try to make it something that it's not. Let's just take our consciousness right through that beautiful, beloved heartness that they are, the beautiful facet of Creator that they are; and now, with your presence, ignite them. Remember, you have the great honor to let them be right. So let's just light it up. Lighting up their heart level more than ever. Matter of fact, wow, you're even speeding up everything that's being spewed, released, processed and dumped, with nothing to do except love them; no answers to try to conjure up, just honoring them dearly, holding them so brilliantly in the beautiful crèche of love that they are.

Chitchat is chitchat; so let's skip all that part. That's why you're just going to let them be right, because getting engaged in it all is going to get nowhere quick anyway, because you don't have anything to defend or justify. It still just is what it is. And now that you're lighting them up more than ever, can you just ask the beautiful, priceless beloved right before you; *"How best can I offer clarity? What can I offer of heart, of love, of clarity, of solutions, that would assist you to feel more at peace, more calm, more open, more vibrant with what is going on?"* You're not asking to be a problem solver, because in truth, there's not a problem. But truthfully; *"How best can I assist to bring you clarity here"*, without letting yourself be given away or taken away and going in circles that get nowhere really quick. Truthfully, out of great love, out of great honor; *"Dear Heart, how best can I offer you clarity, solutions? How best can we come to clarity and solutions about this? How best can we come together with this as we dance through all of creation together?"*

Now you have two heart levels coming together. You have total light beingness lighting up; a lightening up that's dissolving the beautiful mental, emotional, egoic structure that's trying to find something to anchor into. You've already begun to un-anchor the spewing, letting it spiral out, and now you're reconnecting with them; and then as you just simply let the beautiful one be right, you have nothing to offend, defend nor justify, and you definitely do not have a battle to defend or justify, because being right takes a lot of work, a huge amount of justification, and now you're trying to be right for yourself. You're trying to be right for themselves and now you're trying to prove all this stuff that doesn't require proving. Love is not right. Love is not wrong. Love is love. You cannot prove light to be wrong or right. Light is light. Love is love. And you are who you are.

Honoring yourself here, as you are going through this process or this unfoldment with the dear one, is honoring first and foremost that the dear one is not broken; honoring first and foremost that there's not one scattered facet about them. They're un-raveling; they're waking up, stepping up, being stepped up, being woken up while honoring that it's not your business unless you are asked for assistance, asked for clarity; and then from there, becoming okay with their running through a lot. It's not your job to fix anything here because they're not broken. Making it your job to fix is no more different than judging them to be broken, because they're not broken. Then, as they're not broken, you're able to welcome them to walk with you and being able to truthfully, truly connect with them, letting them connect with you, that is totally, thoroughly, completely a marriage of the heart.

When you're honoring one's self you are honoring that everyone around you is running through what they're running through, but yet things are collapsing and collapsing and you are available for them to come forth to ask for assistance; but once again, not because they're broken, but because now you're available for them to ask. Now, honoring yourself is your accessibility for them to be able to locate you.

> *"What about Expecting Behavior to Change...*
>
> *How do I handle my desire for my spouse to change, and their desire to change me?"*

In a relationship of the heart, the most important facet within the relationship is the underlying core of two hearts coming together full force. Now the funniest part here is when a dear one has suggested and wanted you to change, and within your unique evolvement you try suggested changes. I promise you, some suggestions are going to flow for you and some are not going to work for you. Those that do not work for you, or do not work out, are because you are going against yourself; and the ones that do flow and serve you will assist your unique evolvement.

For example, what if one spouse is very neat and puts their clothes in the clothesbasket, cleans up after themself right after cooking and their office desk is always organized. Now, the other spouse is the opposite and they put cleaning up after themself on their *get around to it list*. They leave their dirty clothes on the bathroom and bedroom floor, their office desk and floor have stacks of papers all around and after making dinner they leave the dirty dishes in the sink because they will *get around to it*, and they will clean it up at some point.

What if the very neat spouse says; "*You know honey this is not working for me and I am out of here because you are not organized. You don't pick up after yourself and you leave the kitchen a mess.*" What do any of those things have to do with love? The part that becomes colorful is that there are all these boxes of how it should be done rather than what is. Does it really matter that there is a costume on the bathroom floor or that there are dirty dishes in the sink? Now, if all those things are put on a check-list and if you put all your dirty clothes in the clothesbasket, if you clean up after yourself in the kitchen on a timely basis and if you organize your desk, then you are compatible? These items have nothing to do with love. At the same time if you say nothing, have no frustration and are not holding your breath, it all will change anyway; not because you want it to change or you demand that it changes, rather that the dear brother starts to step into what works best for them. The changes just begin to happen because of the love being emanated exponentially that begins to create complementary changes automatically.

It is a metamorphosis based on what really matters - love - and what doesn't matter. If all the idle stuff is given so much importance, even though it really has none, what happens? It takes dear ones away from their expression of love. As it is given no importance, it all metamorphosizes anyway, and you begin to notice the other dear one is stepping up to do things differently because it complements themselves and most importantly, it complements the whole because it is fluid and love. The dear one who is stepping up and doing things differently by cleaning up after themselves begins to do it because that is more fluid, not because they need to be courteous, nor that it is a rule, nor even a contemplation. It just becomes automatic because it is fluidity. It's definitely not because of rigidity and rules. It is not like *if I don't do it the Universe is going to fall apart and I'll be chastised.* So when you look and explore relationships with yourself and others, you will begin to find that all this meaning is given to things and actions that do not have any meaning; so why would you let it continue to have such an impact within your life-stream?

You may be asking a question here; i.e., when you are in a place of your isness, your presence, how do you make sure another is not taking advantage of you? If you start to feel like another dear one is trying to take advantage of you, you have a choice. You can give yourself away or not. When you start to go against yourself, you are giving yourself away. For example, let's say the dishes are piled up in the sink again or the dirty clothes are spread all over the bedroom or bathroom. If it was affecting the whole and if you are not called to take care of it, ask the other dear one if they would take care of it to assist the fluidity of the whole. This is a state of clarity. You are not going to go against yourself, waiting for the *getting around to it thing,* and all of what is not being done; and it does not mean the Universe is going to fall apart. If it matters, not that it does matter, but if it matters, then let's go ahead and take care of it. When you address the dear one you are not going into combativeness or anger. You are not going into, *you said you would, your job, my job, etc.*, or letting these scenarios build up. You are going to address them from a state of how to complement the whole with fluidity.

When you let the mind and emotions grow and go to extremes, this is when you start to play, *I want, I want, I want,* from another. Is it elements you give from an open heart, or is it elements that you give or don't give because of the emotions and whom has and carries which roles and responsibilities? Giving from a state of open-heartedness, which is natural, is a true gift. Giving because of responsibilities and obligations is not a gift. It is a state of expectations of another. It is either a gift of love or it is not.

For example, if two people are in a relationship of the heart and married, and *Dear One (A)* is always in a state of love and isness throughout this relationship, *Dear One (A)* is offering to *Dear One (B)*, "*I am right here totally accessible and available.*" If *Dear One (B)* is running at opposite extremes, is abrasive and distant, *(B)* is pushing *(A)* away, and being together is becoming eons of work because *(B)* is dishonoring the relationship.

(B) is wanting *(A)* to chase, support and give more, and more, says the egoic arrogance. Now it becomes an odd tango. This is where *(B)'s* heart is shut down and it is no longer a relationship of the heart nor a communion.

From this place, *(A)* knows the issues are not about the true essence of *(B)*. It is about *(B)'s* behavior and *(A)* can start to look at what they are willing to support here. Now *(A)* is not going to keep all this to themselves. They are going to be clear with *(B)* and share things like; *"Dear One, you know I love you with all of my heart. Do you see that these circumstances are not complementing us, nor the whole, so can we please get back on track again?"* If *(B)* says, *"Yes, but it's all you, it's all you";* wow, can you see how much power they are giving you over themselves? *(A)* *"So all right dear heart, I'll be here when you're ready. Let me know - you know when you're done with that. Hey, knock yourself out, but when you want to walk side-by-side with me, just let me a know. I wish you nothing but the best. Have the best bad day possible and let me know when you're done with it and I'll be right over here. I love you dearly regardless. I hope you fling that stuff as hard as you can and you know what, here's a cup of coffee to drink along the way. I love you no matter what and I'll be right over here when you're ready. Not because I'm better, but because if that's where you want to play have a blast; but I'll be over here."*

> *"What about the feeling of being in Survival Mode?*
>
> *What if everything that is presenting keeps me in survival mode because I lost my job, or I can't pay my mortgage, my spouse left me, etc.?"*

Well, what's happing there isn't so much about what's presenting around you or what is not presenting around you. Let's be clear that it's not your mortgage. It's not even your job. Let's also be clear that it's not even your spouse. It's all these levels of an old karmic, archaic, paradigm that you've already superseded. You see, this is where; *Okay, I've lost my house. I've lost my car vehicle. I've lost Scruffy the puppy dog or kitty cat, whatever, however; my offspring are doing this, doing that, so forth and so forth.* Well of course all these archaic paradigms are dissolving, breaking down, collapsing all over the place, because you have totally, innately, exquisitely outgrown it. You're going through such a beautiful dying off and void as you are coming forth, arising, being stepped up and stepping up, (congratulations) moving to such a beautiful new paradigm as you're taking off, taking off in hyper-drive. You see, this is also where your *big guns* are so totally, completely, dynamically, thoroughly taking charge, taking part, covering your back, *I've got you covered,* running forth with you, singing and dancing with you; but also, wow, you're dancing with the whole Universe and saying, *"Goodbye, goodbye, goodbye"* to all of the old.

None of it has to do with lack. None of it has to do with suffering. It most definitely is saying goodbye to all the poverty consciousness, all the limitation about it, because you are saying goodbye to absolutely everything that does not work, that has not worked. You're saying, *"Goodbye, goodbye, goodbye"* to all these facets of creation that have been so, so colorfully wavering. All these facets of creation that have also been so dynamically holding you back from all that is anyway. You're saying, *"Goodbye, goodbye, goodbye"* to all these facets that you've outgrown anyway. But now you're saying, *"Hello, hello, hello,"* stepping up, letting all these physical, dense-matter principles and matrixes within creation dissolve, break apart, break down to complement you as you arise that much faster.

So let's be clear that the mortgages belong to the Universe. Let's also be clear that all these colorful deities, all these colorful journeys, all these colorful metamorphosis, changes, emanations, brilliances - none of it belongs to you. All of it belongs to your *big guns* that have you covered, that are taking heart and running forth to complement you overtime, all for oneself to sing and dance and flourish overtime, to complement you in hyper-drive.

William and Mary's Relationship of the Heart Questions & Answers

Many dear ones have asked, do ask, about the relationship/marriage of the heart of My Angel and myself; *"How did you meet? What is it like to be married to each other? How do you handle conflicts? Do you have conflicts, etc.?"* In this chapter, Mary, my beloved bride, My Angel and I answer these questions. Yet, before we go there, please remember this is not about a William and a Mary, or a Mary and a William. The importance of this chapter within this book is the importance of the following of the heart, without all the conflicts, the contemplations of the mental level, the emotional levels, the doubt of another, the doubt of oneself and the self-inflicted conflicts of another, even a fear of another or a fear of the manifestational worlds.

For you see, when you begin to expand upon, express upon, to let in the beautiful marriage, the beautiful relationship of a heart level expand as an absolute, without reluctancy, it is absolutely right there, available for you; but yet, it is more often pushed away than it is let in. It is more often pushed away and fought off, than it is arisen and embraced and allowed to come to life. It into boxes, trying to fit it into understandings, trying to fit it into all of these colorful parameters of carnality and survival; *This is what I want when I want it. This is how it should be, when it should be. This is how it's not supposed to be. This is what it must be. This is what it must look like. This is how it must work. This is how it must not work. I must be the fearless leader and you must be the fearful follower. This is considered peace. This is not peace. You make me happy. You don't make me happy. Your actions, your behaviors are acceptable, or not acceptable due to my personal filters, judgments, or everything I've been taught.*

When you open your heart levels, you let in the infinite expression, expansiveness, the infinite enjoyment, love, passion, bliss, exquisiteness, without all the busyness, without all the carnality, without all the survival, without all the control, without any control. This is a heart that is totally wide open. You can call it *vulnerable.* You can even call it *accessible*, but most importantly, *available.* Letting your heart level be wide open says; "*Hey, you know what, this is who I am. This who I am and it's who I'm always going to be. This is who I've always been. I am who I am.*" Some will say; "*I am that I am.*" It doesn't really matter what the words are; *I am not broken. I have nothing to be afraid of. I have no rules to follow. I have no dating/mating game to go through, nor all the interviewing processes. I am love. You are love and let's have a blast. I am light. You are light. How best can we shine upon each other? How best can we merge together and celebrate together, quite exquisitely, quite unanimously?* *How best can we complement? How much can we complement?* There is no end. Here is the beloved of your heart in a marriage of the heart. Let's not forget, if you were meant to be alone you would not have a gender. If you were to be alone, you would not have an X or a Y chromosome. Now there are many who have chosen to be celibate. Have a blast; but yet, have a blast without the obsoleteness, without the absoluteness of becoming separated or segregated from the love that you are and being able to express it with another.

Now the premise and importance of this book is its *How-To-s:* how to live without self-doubt, without holding back; how to have the courage to let yourself be wide open, accessible and available enough to let yourself have everything; how to let yourself dance with everything and everyone. And the most important *how-to* of all; how to allow the intimacy, the exquisiteness, the elegance, the pricelessness of letting another heart, another facet of Creator Incarnate come to you and literally merge right through you. There is nothing to hide. *I am who I am.* There is nothing to hide. There is nothing to pretend. There are no schematics. There is nothing to run from. There is no rulebook that says, "*Okay, when this happens that can happen.*" There is no too fast. There is no too slow. There is no certain pathway where everyone has to be on their tiptoes. There is no thin ice or thick ice that you have to walk on. But it is with courage - I want to add - for the mental level and for oneself, to have the passionate openness and flourishment to let all of oneself be thoroughly, completely exposed to oneself - which is the easy part –

while letting oneself be completely exposed to another; the vulnerability, the exquisiteness, the wide-openness and the total complete vulnerability to let another heart begin to merge with yours, letting yours merge with them.

So what happens when you play with the importance of the premise within this book; *How best can we merge with another?* You're not taking on debris, but emanating the love and the marriage of the heart without becoming afraid. You're superseding all the realms, all the parallels, all the perceptional dynamics that have been such a beautiful holding back. You have been trying to hide; you have kept secret what you have perceived to not be okay about yourself. Wow, isn't that amazing? When in truth, you're not broken. There's nothing to hide from. But how willing are you to let everything be exposed, without judging it and without being judged? It's called, *The Vulnerability of Your Heart.*

Our Relationship of the Heart - Questions asked by Many Dear Ones:

"How did you and William meet? What was it like?"

Mary:

It was the first day of February 2003 when I first met Will. I had been invited to a gathering being held in a home here in Las Vegas. My friend who invited me was very excited about it. Her enthusiasm was contagious. All she could really tell me is that Will was very different – a matrix. He did not date, lived a quiet life, worked a lot and was extremely different than anyone else. I think the *matrix* part intrigued me the most. I decided to go and meet Will to see what I thought.

As I was driving there, I noticed that it was an unusually beautiful, very warm day for the first of February - a very bright sunny day. I thought that it might be a little odd of me, coming to this huge home full of people who were so spiritually evolved. I didn't feel very evolved myself. When I pulled up to find a parking place I did not see my friend's car. I knew she had not yet arrived. Normally I would have had second thoughts about walking in by myself, but this day I didn't. I knew I had to be there.

As I was listening to him speak I was amazed by William Linville. He spoke much more quickly back then, and I started to wonder if everyone was getting everything that Will was speaking about on a mind level. I knew I did not absorb all of it, not by a long shot, but I knew that was okay. I found out this was Will's first public speaking engagement. I would have guessed he had done many previously. Everything just flowed so easily and perfectly. I had never experienced this type of energy before. When Will finished speaking I signed a sheet so someone could call me to schedule a session. I could not imagine what it would be like. I just knew I must schedule a session with Will and I knew it would be most beneficial.

I noticed many people were leaving. Many were going to a backyard patio. I started to leave, but as soon as I started to open the door to make my exit, a psychic who was there asked me why I didn't stay awhile and come out on the patio. *Why not?* I thought. Everyone who came outside was given five minutes to connect with Will individually. I felt my five minutes were very special; but everyone did, I am sure. Will gave me his cell phone number and told me he would be in San Diego for the week, but to call him. I didn't know then that Will had been seeing me in my light-realms for three years. When I was driving home I thought about William Linville. I wondered how he ever got a break if he was giving his phone number to everyone. I did not call him that week and just waited for my session. I didn't want to disturb him. I had no idea he had not offered his phone number to anyone else.

I had my session with Will and it was much more than I expected. That was such an amazing day; I can't even describe what it felt like. When I got home I had to stay outside. I took my computer with me, but could not stop looking at the sky. I was seeing beautiful colors and images I had never been able to see before. I was surprised a few days later when I got a call from the person who was handling promotions for Will at the time. Will asked her to call me to see if I would like to meet at Starbucks for a coffee. He wanted to talk about scheduling other gatherings here in Las Vegas. I was very happy, very much looking forward to having coffee with Will, but I did not know why he had invited me.

I was pulling up to Starbucks and there he was. All of a sudden, something really hit me. He looked so beautiful sitting there in his white shirt, black shorts, sandals and sunglasses. He was talking on his cell phone. I suddenly had this amazing, strong attraction to Will. But I remembered that he did not date. I did not realize it then, but what I was feeling was more than a strong physical attraction, what I was feeling was a true marriage of the heart. Over the course of having coffee and visiting, I mentioned I would like to host one of his gatherings in my home. I told him I knew a lot of people who would love to come. I invited Will over to dinner so we could talk further. We had dinner and talked; later we had Swiss cheese and crackers and talked some more.

Once Will came to dinner, he never left. He brought over his three boxes and moved in the next day. My friend who had invited me to the gathering called me soon after that. She had developed a huge crush on William Linville. It was difficult for me to tell her that Will had moved into my home, that it was now *our* home. She could only get past the feelings she had for him once she understood *what* she was feeling from him. I had to explain Will to her, the total unconditional love and no judgment – pure love. She had never had that experience from another human. Most of us have only experienced that feeling with our animals. Once I was able to explain to her, she was able to move forward much more quickly in her work with Will. She was able to step it up, to stay on track with her journey of opening and expanding. She was able to allow the love for what it is.

And that's the way it was for everyone who met Will. The small gathering I hosted at our house was a great success. Everyone I invited came to see Will. They were very grateful for their invitations, and they all became clients. Life was amazing for us - unbelievable actually. And then my mind started to kick in. You know, the little voice that says if something seems too good to be for real, it probably is. I started feeling a little cautious.

One night after we'd been together about four months, Will invited me to dinner. We had reservations at Alizé, the restaurant at the Top of the Palms. Will asked me to dress up. He had purchased a beautiful new blue suit to wear. When we arrived, there was a bottle of champagne on the table. He had purchased the most beautiful glass vase I had ever seen and it was filled with red roses. Right away, Will got down on his knee, opened a box with an incredible ring he had designed, and proposed to me. I was so excited, so happy, and so full of love for this beautiful man! I said, *Of course I will marry you!* I felt so much joy. But later that little mind-chatter started going again. I thought about his proposal for a day or so, and finally told him I thought we should wait for about a year. If everything was still as amazing and perfect, I would love to marry him. And that is exactly the way it played out.

I found it was not only possible, but natural, to have a true marriage of the heart with no conflicts. I realized that there are times when things are just what they seem to be, and there's no other 'shoe to drop.' Over the course of the next few weeks, I brought up a few things to discuss that were preying on my mind. I had noticed how neat and organized Will was, and how not so neat and disorganized I was. I would find my makeup put away before I had used it. The memory of that always makes me smile. I thought Will might get tired of me, especially my disorganization. I was wrong. Different doubts kept coming up in my mind and then leaving as I learned to feel with my heart and keep my mind out of the way. When Will said, *"All is perfect,"* he really meant it. And it was, and is, and always will be perfect and divine.

Now Will and I dance and sing and share all the love in the Universe. The love grows every day. Life is fun. Sharing life and love is the best. Our marriage of the heart grows every day as well. As far as I am concerned, there are no other men on the planet. This can be your life too, if you can just let each other be. Simply let each other be and you will find that you do not have conflicts. Just love (don't judge), but love unconditionally. Love every day; enjoy your precious time. Let it be easy and fluid. Have a Blast!

William:

Expanding upon what My Angel just shared, when we had our coffee date, it was quite beautiful, quite astounding actually, and peculiar. There were these passionate feelings of love, light-beingness and the only thing that existed was My Angel and the love that emanated (and continues to emanate). My beautiful, passionate bride recognized the eminence, the omnipotence; but yet, the sweetness, the purity, all the way from the event where My Angel was stepping right into her own light-beingness. And beyond her stepping into it - wow - she was already there. On that first meeting I saw My Angel stepping forth. It was automatically the love, the infinite love that has just continued to grow, and grow, and grow.

That coffee date was really quite peculiar, unique and astronomical for me, because My Angel had no need. She was healthy, whole and complete as always; nor did she have any desire except what was growing and developing. For myself it was the same; there was no need, there was no desire, there was no searching. Our heart levels were already married before we ever came together in the physical. All was, and is, astronomical. She arrived for the coffee and – wow! The passion just took off and grew and grew and grew. We were communicating beyond the physical. After I left that coffee, I was heading to San Diego for a week, and she brought me a beautiful basket full of goodies for me to take on my trip.

The love took place automatically. There was no holding on or holding back, not even during the week that I was, let's say, physically absent. There was no lack. There wasn't all this colorful, emotional hoopla and so forth. There was only a constant growing of love. And yet, it was instantaneous – no filters, no buffers, no ifs, ands, or buts. There was no *I wonder if, could be, maybe, possibly, should be, shouldn't be, it's meant to be.* There was none of this quite colorful, emotional, idle chitchat. It was literally; *There she is, let's go!* Everything, and I do mean **everything**, took off and flew omnipotently, exponentially, even to the divine presence of a jeweler. I was working across town at Peccole Ranch, upstairs in a room called the Star Room. One day as I was leaving, there was the jeweler downstairs. Now, I hadn't planned on finding a jeweler, hadn't even thought of a jeweler; the jeweler just presented for me. So I designed a ring, drew it up, and ordered it - done deal.

There was not a contemplation and there is no contemplation; *There's My Angel, let's go!* It was My Angel right before me, just as she had been presenting three years prior. There was no contemplation. What was there to wait around for? There wasn't the dancing, the romancing and all this fun stuff required to know. It was and is instantaneous. There wasn't the dating/mating game. There wasn't all the *socializational protocol.* Now, to say that we have had a lot of beautiful, passionate, romantic dates and so forth, well absolutely; but it wasn't based in statutes of the rulebooks based in humanity's terms. There were no rules. The hearts were already married. The rest, even when I made an extravagant picnic for my bride, these were all gifts of love, gifts of the heart. This was what I would call normal; but let's not forget, I'm healthy, whole and complete, and so is my bride.

Now remember there was no lack, there was no need, there wasn't even a desire on either one of our parts because neither one of us were lacking. Neither one of us was desiring anything. We were not searching. For example, I love what My Angel shares so beautifully about the purchase of her new home. When she found it three months prior to our coming together, her comment was, "*What a beautiful, romantic home. I love this home, even though I'll only be sharing it with myself.*"

Those were her comments, having no idea that I was about to present in her life-stream.

You see, now we're playing with the true marriage of the heart and a Universal gift that's accessible and available for all concerned. But once again, we're playing with nothing held back, and because there is nothing held back, we're letting ourselves receive everything. You see love is love is love. There is no conflict with love. There is total uniquedness, omnipotence. Yet all the uniquednesses of all the facets that are being offered to you are harmonious. *But what about diversities of love?* Well that's where things become a little bit colorful, because everything is love, in so many different forms.

Diversities occur when we start to create all these different formats and forms, rather than live in the fluidity of a uniqued unfoldment of that marriage of the heart. There are no buffers. There are no variables. There are no barriers. There's no waiting game. Really, it becomes; *there it is, let's go.* There are no interviewing processes, no resumes, so forth and so forth. You're playing with you and the whole Universe. But yet, you're playing with everyone, everything being presented for you, around you, so uniquedly, so brilliantly, to let the hearts come together instantaneously.

Now as My Angel was sharing, there were no other male structures on the planet for her. Well, as far as I was concerned, was there another feminine structure on the planet? No. Because, quite literally speaking, divinely, Universally speaking, really on every level, before My Angel arrived into my life-stream, there had never been a feminine structure on the planet. As far as I'm concerned, there's still not a feminine structure on the planet. There's My Angel in all her beautiful, priceless, divine feminine presence, which I love so dearly. And My Angel is total complete love.

You see, the notion of a femininity is so overrated. In My Angel I see the total complete presence of divinity, heart level passion, exquisiteness and such a beautiful physicality. The love she emanates, the exquisite passion she emanates is exquisitely divine. There are a lot of priceless dear brothers on their journeys, but My Angel is my exquisite, benevolent bride because of who she is. This is not about a structure. It's not about a gender. It's about My Angel. It's about the love that we are fully, completely expressing together. This goes beyond being preordained; it becomes about being completely, naturally, exquisitely, passionately merged with another. There's only one Mary Elizabeth. And what we celebrate every day, beyond space and time - what we celebrate eternally, externally, expressively, unanimously - is untouchable. Isn't it amazing how it grows, moment by moment? There's nothing comparable to where we began, to where we're at right now and where we're going to be eons from now. And how do we affect the planetary matrix, the Universe? There's a whole other journey from there that is exquisitely, exponentially lighting everything up.

Is our relationship based in a script? Is it based in all of these thoughts of *meant to be, have to be* and contracts? Absolutely not! It's expressive, unanimously, eternally, permanently constantly growing. The only conflict we've ever had is who loves the other more; and it's a fun conflict, because it's not really a conflict. It's an exquisite, complete presence that we have great humor with. Our love never has had, and never will have anything to do with searching. It's has everything to do with the lack of looking, the lack of lacking, because we lack of nothing – never have, never will. It has everything to do with willingness to share everything, to express everything and beyond that there are no barriers, no filters, no boundaries. There's one heart married together, exquisitely and unanimously.

Our love goes well beyond vulnerability, too. There are no secrets. Why would we have a secret from love? How can you have a secret from love? We share everything, because what is there not to share? Communication is a walk in the park because what is there not to share when it's all love? What is there not to exquisitely express, exponentially, when it's all gold, it's all love? There is no holding back. What is there to sacrifice when there is no sacrifice, because it's all love? What is there not to exquisitely expand upon when it's all love? What compromises are there when there are no compromises? It all comes back full circle to no wavering, no boundaries, no barriers, because it's of the heart - from the total complete marriage of the higher through the lower, from a total complete expressiveness. There is no right; there is no wrong, because how can one be right or wrong when it's all love anyway?

And it's a love that's untouchable. It's a love that is un-taint-able. It's a love that is un-measurable. Funny enough, to both of our head-scratchings, it's a love that constantly grows. Even when it seems like it can't possibly grow further, it always does. Even when it seems sooo amazing, it always grows – expands upon, expands upon, expands upon and expands upon itself. Even by the time this book comes out, it will have compounded about 798 times. Once again, it is not affectable because it constantly metamorphosizes and grows.

Relationships become so humorous due to the trivial, the superficial level of the carnal levels, and all that silly stuff. We'll call it *gender principles*. Now, what if everyone were to supersede all the gender stuff, the masculine and the feminine. What if the *Who does what, when, how, where and why* didn't exist? Could you imagine what would take place within your life-stream? Can you imagine what your whole life-stream would be like if you simply brought things back into the perspective of the most important thing? What if you chose Universal, unanimous love?

The heart is the core, the key to everything, to your own existence. The heart is love. That's what fuels life force everywhere - love, which is the heart. That's what creates the marriage of the heart - love's light-beingness. It is gold, gold, gold. It's a presence, a presence beyond just a feeling. It is an emanation beyond a thought. It is a beautiful state that fuels manifestation. It even fuels what you would call the perceptions of a reality. Love is the core of creation before creation was brought into a manifestational form. It wouldn't matter if my bride was a male or a female. My bride is my bride because of the love we exquisitely express together.

My bride has brought to me at times, *Well, Honey, you know if I ever left the physical, I would want you to have another partner.* I thank her so much for her thoughtfulness. I really mean it with every particle of my being. That is so, so beautifully thoughtful, so caring, so kind. Yet my response is always the same; *Sweetheart, I have no interest.* I don't say that to be kind. I say that because there's truly no interest. Our love is not single. It's not individual. It's expressive. Because before My Angel, the beloved of my heart was ever presented in my life-stream, there was no interest. I am still healthy, whole and complete on my own, because I, and the whole Universe as one, have no need. I had no interest until there was my bride. The marriage of the heart has nothing to do with a replacement plan. It's the presence of love that fuels everything, because I and my beloved are one. How is there ever a need when there's a marriage of the heart? And isn't this also true for you? As you have no need, you have everything. As you have no lack, you have the Universe.

> *"How can it be possible that you have no conflicts? How is that possible?"*

Mary:

Most people have conflicts over money, relationships, children, and all kinds of different things. And I just say that there is no need. Once you develop the marriage of the heart and get the mind out of the way, you can love each other and not judge each other. Let each other be who you are, who you were meant to be. Don't try to change each other, and you won't have the conflicts.

William:

I often address these colorful levels of: *How can you have no conflicts? How is it possible not to have conflicts about finances, physical separation, doubts or questions of trust - even the form of the relationship?* Well, what is there to have conflicts over when you let abundance be abundance? Conflict is all on the outside world anyway. Abundance is a dance, a relationship, a passionate dance, a fluidity dance. What is there to have a conflict about when you let abundance be abundance? What is there to have conflicts about when you let the family monad be the family monad? What is there to have conflicts about when you honor another's partnership, a marriage of the heart? What is there to have conflict about when you're honoring a dear brother in their journey as well, honoring what's presenting for the other dear one as if it were yourself? *Great! Have a blast dear brother; we're together anyway.*

When I'm flying here or flying there on an airplane, or driving here, driving there, for a day or a weekend, it doesn't matter what it is, isn't our love still love? My bride is always presenting from her light-realms anyway. So is yours. So is your partner's, so is every thing. And if that's the case, what is there to have conflict about? It may be what is happening around you, but it doesn't have anything to do with you. The family monad has nothing to do with you. Abundance has nothing to do with you. It's still outside of you. It still has nothing to do with your heart level. We all love, honor and love dearly, but you know, really, what is there to have a conflict over?

Sometimes I'll share with My Angel, *Sweetheart, after work today, with all these markers, all these sequences of events, let's go to the movies.* Or I'll say, *Sweetie, I'm going to go to Red Rock Canyon. Would you like to come?* Interestingly, her reply is sometimes, *Sweetheart, would you rather go alone, or would you like me to come along with you?* Now, isn't that a little bit different? My Angel is really asking, *Sweetie, would you like some 'Will Time' or would you like a hot date? What would you like Sweetheart?*

Is that kind of surprising? Well, remember, My Angel is healthy, whole and complete. She knows that she lacks nothing. She doesn't doubt our love. She doesn't doubt me; she honors and trusts me. She knows me well enough to know that I may want to take some *Will Time.* We call it *Mary Time* and *Will Time.* My Angel may want to go to Macy's, or she may want to take a train to Tennessee. She may want to go across town. She may simply want to take down time away from everybody, including me. She may, she may, she may; but yet, it's always a mutual honoring - regardless, it's always a dance.

My bride may go here or there. She may want this or she may what that. She may want to visit a family member. I may be called to do phone sessions. Maybe I want to go to Red Rock Canyon. I may prefer to go to California. I might decide, for some odd reason, to go to Texas or somewhere. Great. We say, *Have a blast, Sweetheart, and I'll see you when I get back.* We're like this because we're always together anyway. Our hearts are always married anyway. And you see, the conflicts come with the concept that physically, you're supposed to be together side-by-side. Conflict comes with, W*ell, I don't know if I can trust this dear one.* That's all mental hoopla. It's all perceptional belief systems. The part that's so often forgotten when conflicts arise is love. It's called love and honor. *All right, Sweetheart, I'm healthy, whole complete and so are you. So have a blast and I'll see you back at the palace when you return.*

You see, once again, we're both healthy, whole and complete. We'll do what we do, go where we go. We're always together from our light-realms. It's always a mutual honoring, and when we're back from our adventures we'll go out and have what we call, a *Romantic Dinner Date*, or a *Coffee Date.* We may end up doing Red Rock together. We may go to the movies together. We may even sit here in the palace just enjoying the omnipotence together. It doesn't matter if we're counting the rocks in the yard or playing with our kitty-cats. It's not what we're doing. It's who we are. It's the presence that we share together.

"Do you ever plan at all for the future?"

Mary:

Yes, of course we do. We both have retirement accounts and we invest. For example, we plan on turning our current palace into a beautiful, romantic rental home for a special couple when we move into our new palace.

William:

Yes we play with investing and enjoy all the beautiful splendor of playing with these systems and all of brother humanity. We have retirement accounts and I have to laugh because when we selected them we were given three options; high risk, low risk and no risk. So we selected all three just for fun. We have rental properties and we are moving into our next palace. The new palace will allow us to play further with more space to do our webcasts, more space for me to walk around while assisting, and a new variety of space for us to play in. But this does not mean we are going to retire when we reach a certain age, and it does not mean we are trying to win with capital gains to create financial abundance. It does mean that when the different markers arrive we will have new endeavors and the tools to play with them, dance with them and enjoy them.

Most importantly, we are playing. We are enjoying and we are lighting up the planetary grid system as we have a blast playing with investing, as we have a blast with all that comes our way. Whatever we play with, we are still lighting up the planetary matrix as we enjoy the economic realms. The love is always constant, even with all of these metaphoric future financial potentials. The part I love the most is we get to affect so many different life-streams that much further, because we are more accessible and available than ever. Whether we hire a painter or purchase filming equipment, whatever we play with affects so many dear ones' life-streams. We enjoy all the Universe has to offer and more.

"When a couple has a business together it is often difficult to leave it all behind. How do you get away from it all?"

Mary:

We get away from our business quite often in lots of different ways. We have our drives through Red Rock Canyon. We have our wonderful coffee dates at different Starbucks around town; our favorite being the one where we had our first date. We have numerous nights away throughout the year at one of the local resorts, and we take short trips to some of our favorite places in Utah, Arizona and California. We use these times to get away from it all and break energy with work and play with each other in all these different locations, with different conversations about all the diversities of our lives.

William:

We also turn off all the phones to take-five from streams of consciousness and accessibility, even though dear ones still do present from their higher levels. We will go to all the beautiful, priceless places My Angel mentioned and we will be in our palace thoroughly enjoying each other. I wouldn't call it *getting away*. If I were to give it a name, I would call it *thoroughly and exquisitely embracing the constant unfoldment and blossoming of diversities of life*. There really is no way to take-five from the Universe. Why would you want to? The more you let love be love and follow your heart and your light-beingness, the more of a blast you will have with everything and everyone. You say, "*Here it is, let's go,*" without contemplating and questioning. By just welcoming and going with what is here for you, you will never, ever be without.

There is no contemplation needed about anything. *Is it love-based or not? Is it assisting the whole, or is it about a me-me-me?* This is where so many get conflicted and misconstrued. *Is it the heart, or is it the mind?* Well, it comes down to one thing, is it love-based or is it not? Love is love is love. Yet there is never a lack when it comes to a relationship of the heart, a marriage of the heart. It is a constant that continues to grow. There is never a lack; there is a constant expansiveness.

> *"How and to what effect does your relationship affect others and vice versa?"*

Mary:

Will and I regularly receive emails and comments from people. Some are in a loving relationship, and some are hopeful it is possible they can have a marriage of the heart. Some comment that based on seeing, feeling and hearing about our relationship, they now know it is possible for them to find their own marriage of the heart. Some have a dear one that they love very much, but for some reason they have been struggling in their relationship. They notice that through seeing and feeling our relationship, their relationship starts to become easier and they express a lot more love together.

As far as the relationships of others, when I see other couples exude love, happiness and joy in their relationship, it automatically brings us a great deal more joy.

William:

Through our relationship, dear brothers feel such a profound love, an intimate, infinite and passionate love - such a huge honoring and an infinite, intimate connectedness. Some get very challenged. Some go into tears. For some there's a deep sigh of relief. For some, there is a deep yearning of; *I knew it, I knew it, I knew it. I knew it was possible, and there it is. I know it's possible, and there it is.* Others are so elated, they say, *"Thank you, thank you, thank you"* and then they ask, *"How do we get there?"* Still others will humorously, but somewhat seriously, ask My Angel if I ever give out DNA samples or if I have relatives. Now I have to be clear; these requests are not about a William. They've simply never seen love like this before. And in truth, for both My Angel and myself, this is not about a William and a Mary. It's about an *Us*.

For the ones who literally break down in tears, it's because the love and light-beingness emanating moves right through them. They become speechless. What is happening is elation for them. It's elation and expansiveness, an expressiveness and a wide openness for them. That is the most important part here – both the masculine and feminine structures say; *"I too can go here. This is available to me."* So many dear ones get so affected their hearts open just like that.

Others get so challenged. Because remember, they've attempted to be in such domination of how a relationship should be, and that's okay. Let's celebrate how a male structure should behave and how a feminine structure should behave. Yet the part that becomes peculiar is when they push it for everything it is worth, from an old paradigm, and it challenges their whole life-stream. It challenges their whole world; challenging their current relationships, their past, present and future. We are lighting them up from the outside and the inside, and from the inside through the outside. It is My Angel and I expanding and expanding exponentially without trying. It's natural. It's the love that's expressed, that collapses all the barriers, that diffuses all the conflicts and challenges for dear ones.

You, too, are capable of doing this. More importantly, you collapse these barriers yourself when you lack nothing; *I am who I am. Let's go.* You are doing it more and more when you doubt nothing; *There it is. I am ready.* You do this not from a mental level, but totally from a heart level.

Let's not make all these decisions about oneself, about a relationship. Let's just come to terms with your own light-beingness; *I am ready to be open for everything. I lack nothing. I need nothing. I am okay being alone. I'm okay being with others too. I am not afraid of others. I am not afraid of myself. I'm not afraid at all. I am fine, and I can laugh to myself, out loud and otherwise just for the sake of laughing. I can enjoy just for the sake of enjoying. As a matter of fact, I'm even my own best friend. I can even tell myself jokes and laugh at my own jokes, just because I'm fine.*

Now, as you are playing here, you're opening and opening and opening; becoming healthy, whole, complete – truly vibrant. You are also expanding exponentially within a relationship with the beloved of your heart, in a marriage of the heart, but also with yourself and everyone else. Relationships have a life of their own. So why stifle the life? Let's watch how all of it opens and opens and opens big time. As with My Angel and myself, let's watch all the life forms you affect, all the dynamics you affect.

My Angel and I were up in Seattle once with another couple. They were such a blast and we were really enjoying our time with them. When we were on our way to the train station one of them said, *"Well, don't you guys ever argue?"* And the dear brother who was driving looked in the rear view mirror and said, *"Will, don't you ever just get frustrated?"* So My Angel and I decided to have some fun with this and pretended to argue about our train tickets. She pretended not to have the train tickets, and I pretended to be upset: *Oh honey, you always forget this, you always forget that!* And we kept on and on and on. At that point, you could hear the wheels rolling in their minds like the tires rolling on the asphalt. They were totally shocked. We could see how they were withdrawing and withdrawing as everything was unfolding, going so fast. Suddenly we chuckled, and *Woosh!* The car lit up brighter than ever. Now that's a great example of how you can affect others. When they feel your love, they light up brighter, more vibrant than ever. Their life-streams open up, and their relationships open up.

Now, when I'm being asked the vice versa level of how other relationships affect us, for myself, they don't. I honor where dear brothers are at within their life-streams. I watch what's going on. I watch what's going on behind closed doors. I watch what's going on within their personal, uniqued life-streams. I watch what's going on in their life-stream as a whole, but I also watch everything that's happening and unfolding. I have two states about myself; neutrality, which is still love, omnipotence and brilliance; and exuberance, which is neutrality and having a blast overtime. Now technically speaking, it's one state really. You have neutrality, and even when you engage you have neutrality.

So, engagement is having a blast, but I'm always engaged and I'm always neutral, and I'm always presented with what's going on here and there. I'm looking at this, looking at that, being presented with this and that, going into life-stream upon life-stream. So, I'd have to say other relationships do not have an impact because it's not my business. But still I'm emanating right through them and really showing and sharing with dear ones what they too can have within their life-streams. *Bring it on.* You are natural. You're exquisitely divine. So why don't you begin to just let your heart levels open up? I'm not talking about opening up from a fluffy state, because then you're just playing head-games with yourself. Why don't you give yourself the courage to hold nothing back? Why don't you just begin by letting your heart level open up and simply give yourself the courage to hold nothing back?

> *"How does the evolution of your relationships with others, as well as those from beyond the veil, affect your physicality?"*

Mary:

It affects me a lot. Depending on the frequency of the vibrational levels of others, I can feel my own levels change. Around certain people I've felt my vibrational levels go down. Then there are people, special family members and friends, and most of all Will, who help lift up my vibrational levels. This has an amazingly wonderful effect on my physicality. It just brings me a lot of comfort, joy, happiness and smiles.

You ask about the vibrational levels of those beyond the physical. This question brought to mind the time when Will first moved in. He would tell me constantly of all the dear ones hanging out with us in our home. Back then I thought it was a little odd to have so many visitors, especially in our bedroom. The visitors are still here and now it's perfectly wonderful with me that they're all here, all these wonderful essences throughout our house. I hope they have a lot of fun being here with us. I think they must, because they stay and they bring their friends.

William:

In the evolvement of our relationship with others, it doesn't have any effect upon me, but it is constantly raising the vibratory levels of other dear brothers. My vibratory levels continue to metamorphosize and they anchor in, as do yours. Once your vibratory levels reach a certain state - let's say 153,000 megahertz per second - that is where they're going to anchor in. They never go back and anchor in any lower. They anchor in at the highest peak, so as a marker that I'm playing with right now, my vibratory levels are at a base level of 1,998,300 megahertz per second, and then this evening, this afternoon, they will spike higher. These levels are going to go higher and anchor in again. The same occurs for you at a rate that is most complementary to your uniqued isness and physicality.

Now from here, regardless of who I am around, what's going to happen is that their body's vibratory levels are going to rise and rise and rise. That just is what it is. My vibratory levels are going to be hugely affecting the dear ones around me. Let's be clear, other dear brothers are going to be where they're going to be. So, let's honor the dear brothers. Let them share what they want to share. Let's just let them be where they're at, densified, whatever it may be, doom and gloom, whatever. But in a relationship, for a moment, can we please not try to change them? Can we just let them have a blast with the doom and gloom in the world, and the sky is falling and everything else? Can we please just have fun with it? Let's just honor that their sky is falling. Let's just honor that the earth is going to collapse, the governmental parties are going to take over finance, so forth and so forth. Can we just let them be where they're at? Let's not 'allow' them. That takes way too much work. Let's just really enjoy the party. Let's not do anything about it, because that's where you're starting to get hooked-in. Let's just enjoy the show.

So now can you just run forth and run forth, just playing with your vibratory levels and how much faster you're letting yourself fly and flourish. And let's watch the evolvement, because remember as you're not getting hooked-in, you're not getting hijacked, you're not even trying to challenge, change and do all this fun stuff for the dear ones. You aren't trying to save them. It doesn't matter who they are - friends, family monads, or so forth. Let's just really, let them be where they're at, believe whatever they want to believe in, get hooked-in, get wrapped up in where ever they at.

But let's not get wrapped up into it. Let's honor where they are with everything. And from here, let's let your selves arise and arise. Let's watch this evolvement, this evolution. Let's watch how very quickly this firm ground under other dear brothers, that they are attempting to stand on, becomes like beach sand. Just watch how all that anchored-in debris starts to slide right through their fingers, how it starts to break down and break apart very fast, literally very fast. But remember, you're not going to get involved. You're just going to enjoy the show, because you're playing with evolvement here, and watch how quickly dialogues, conversations and even relationships start to change. All of it starts changing its track. Let's just let it take on its own life without getting involved.

Now, let's take it further. Because remember, in a relationship level, it's a dance back and forth, letting the dear brothers come forth to you. Remember, no one is broken here so let's enjoy the dance. Let's watch how quick, how fast, how unanimously they start coming forth, how even the dialogue starts to metamorphosize and change. And now, as we're playing with what we'll call the angelic, archangelic and ascended host realms, look at how fast you're going the faster things are changing here too. The part that's often not visited here is how much you're assisting and affecting these dear brothers. Because remember, the faster your vibratory levels are going, the faster you're waking up, running forth and flourishing. You are so omnipotently, divinely opening up portholes for these dear brothers so they can what we'll call evolve, amplify, radiate and run forth too. Because let's not forget, love is love is love; transcendence, transition, evolution and evolvement - ascension - is waking up and taking off, too.

When we play with your vibratory levels for a minute - the speed in which the body's calibration latticework vibrates in megahertz - we're speeding things up. You see now, you are affecting the angelic, archangelic, ascended host realms and your guidance realms, so now we're really playing with the beautiful relationships. Now, we're opening up portholes for yourself and your physicality, which in turn is opening up portholes for these dear brothers, and your physicality is becoming more agile, more mobile, more fluid, more energetic and vibrant. We're playing with everything, communicating, re-writing, with permanent physical metamorphoses happening. All is opening, expanding, expressing to complement you as you run forth. Now, as this is all happening, let's be clear, your physicality is stepping up, stepping up, stepping up, to be able to complement you and to be enjoyed as well. Because from here, your body principal is speeding up, speeding up, speeding up, and *Wow!* – jamming faster and faster, flourishing faster and faster and faster – in hyper-drive.

So now, your body principal is starting to complement you even more. It's starting to radiate, emanate, re-write and move through such a beautiful re-gestation period to complement you overtime, to allow you to take off overtime. You're letting your angelic, archangelic, ascended host realms, and our guidance realms complement you and talk with you further. You're also letting the relationships around you - loved ones, friends, family monads and so forth - grow and grow and grow. So much to share with dear brothers, to remind them, to steer, journey, teach and guide. Well we've really turned the tables on this one. It goes beyond letting dear brothers be where they're at. You're no longer supporting where they're at, and you're letting them come forth to you.

In Closing

My Angel and I love you dearly. And relationships are not the work that has been taught and taught and taught. Actually a relationship is the absence of work. But just for your own clarification, when you try to make a relationship work, have you noticed how many walls you build? Rather than letting your relationship be the beautiful flower that it is, that constantly blooms and blossoms, the petals start to fall. When you integrate your vibratory levels, you integrate. I call it *stabilize*. There's no drop; you keep going and going. You may try to drop, you may play in little cesspools of consciousness just to show yourself they don't work; regardless here comes the next blossom, we'll call it more irradiation, changes and amplification. Any way we look at it, you have more opening and opening, amplifications, wide openness, communion, the heart level opening, flourishing, connecting, marrying, merging faster than ever. But then those petals are going to fall and a whole new iridescence opens up and then here comes the whole bouquet; it's going to integrate, amplify and anchor in. It's going to be the most beautiful bouquet that continues to flourish, and then sure enough, surprisingly enough, all of that falls away, dies away, and now here comes another one, that goes well beyond a beautiful bouquet, we're going into a whole garden; and the garden takes off and takes off and sure enough, no weeding is necessary. Then that garden dies off, but now we have a whole continent of gardens, and then they die off and now we have a whole planet of gardens, then we have a whole Universe, then we have Universes beyond this Universe; and then we have all that is, that there's no end to, because - love is love is love. There's only a beginning. There is no end.

We love you dearly,
William and Mary

Appendix A:

The Difference between Watching and Observing

Watching is a total and complete disengaged state, letting everything truly and completely go where it goes, grow where it grows, watching everything that is going on around from an overview, with total and pristine divine clarity. It is a state where you are unaffected emotionally by all the different scenarios going on around you while you are right in the midst of it all. You are not withdrawing nor protecting oneself as you are playing with everything and you are immune to any drama playing out around you. You are not trying to fix someone who is not broken, nor are you in overwhelm and fighting with the perceptions of the head level.

Observation is where you are still engaged with your head level as you observe an event; questioning, analyzing, judging and making decisions about behavioral mannerisms of yourself and others, and then moving towards being either better than or less than, or these events equals this first, etc.

Observing is an open door for; "*I've got to stand my ground and you have to stand your ground. I am going make my line of death. I can only handle so much; you are going to cross it or attempt to cross it, or back off from it, and now I am in charge*", says the egoic structure. "*I am justified for my reactions, because the other dear brother put me in that scenario, and remember that this is all their doing, all their fault.*" In observing, you and the heart level are missing. It is the head watching the other heads and behaviors and attempting to control the head.

And now you might try to take the higher road and observe the others behavioral mannerisms under the Universal magnifying glass of your egoic expectations, of what they should do and not do. You're going to observe and observe all their issues and let your frustrations with them build up within you, knowing that you are the dominant overseer of this relationship as you are more gifted; and as your frustrations build, your dragons get so much stronger and awaiting to attack these other brothers. As you are the dominant one, you are going to fix all these different dynamics because you know all the things that are wrong with the dear ones. You might allow and allow the other dear ones, because that is what you are supposed to do, while all along, you are making the list in the conscious and sub-psyche of everything they are not doing or doing wrong. You are building up your battle plan; for when it comes time to crucify, you have a lot of justifiable reasons for why you are going to put the stakes in.

Or you could just honor and celebrate where they are at on the ascending journey, their journey of waking up to transcendence and so much more. Or you could just watch without stakes and the other dear brother can be the divinity that they are and the fluidity that they are. As you are arising, they are arising and the love is flowing and flowing, expanding, expanding, etc.

Appendix B:

Judgment - Empathy and Sympathy

Empathy and sympathy are no different than energetically taking the dear brother on, pulling them into you. This is when you start to feel for others, which is no different than taking them on and putting them into a baby carriage and carrying them within your body, rather than walking side-by-side with them. Empathy and sympathy are still judgments. If you feel empathy and sympathy for a dear brother's journey, you are being impacted by their journey. Rather than being your love and light, now you are allowing yourself to be manipulated by them. You are allowing their journey to manipulate you. Manipulation is manipulation, regardless of what the metaphoric behavior is. It is what it is. It is letting oneself be hijacked. It's no different than feeling anger towards a dear one's behavior and taking in the anger and letting it take your love and your light-beingness away. You are judging them and in turn you are allowing yourself to be manipulated by another dear brother's behavior and making it about them rather than the behavior. You are giving them power and control over you. When you get into empathy and sympathy, how is it possible to make an excuse for one without making an excuse for another? This is where things for a dear one get so turned around and the emotions of empathy and sympathy start to cloud and filter your clarity. The mind starts to create justifications that some things are okay and some things are not. You start to make excuses that some dear ones are okay and some are not.

Additionally, when you are in a state of empathy and sympathy for a dear one, you are supporting a dear one's behavior, rather than being the light, and neutrality, and the instrument that you are, which naturally is there to assist them to wake up, run forth and metamorphosize when they are asking. Allow yourself to do an exercise right now: Sit quietly and welcome forth something for which you feel empathy or sympathy. As you do this, watch what happens to your body. Did you notice your body begin to feel drained? Or, did you feel a little void and feel your body become withdrawn and tighten up? Why would you ever feel sorry for, sympathetic, or empathetic for Creator Incarnate?

Let's look at another relationship with a dear one. Let's say it is a familial relationship. You are the brother and your sister has anger conflicts. She verbally takes it out on the family and her children; yet, at the same time loves you and the family dearly. She just can't control her anger. Enter, empathy and sympathy. You feel empathy and sympathy for her because of how your mother treated your sister and at the same time, you feel empathy and sympathy for your sister's children. Now, as you imagine the brother, what do you imagine he is feeling? What is occurring for him?

At a minimum he is feeling more, and more, and more drained every time he thinks of them or is with them. This may continue for the brother's whole life because he keeps feeling empathy and sympathy for his sister, her children and the family - draining and draining the brother more and more because he keeps feeling the pull of empathy and sympathy without focusing on a solution or a direction in which he can place his own feelings. It is a repetitive, cyclical cycle that gets nowhere. Of course the brother could shut that sister out of his life because of how she attempts to make him feel; but then he would feel guilty because he's supposed to be supportive and empathize with her and her children. And now this dear one continues in this repetitive, cyclical cycle of empathy, sympathy, guilt, anger, etc., and doesn't make any changes in his way of perceiving the circumstances. Please remember, compassion is; *Dear Brother, I really wish that wasn't happening. Would you like for it to be different now?*

Looking at the other side of this circumstance, how much of what is occurring with his sister, her children, her behavior, etc., have anything to do with him? It doesn't have anything to do with him. He is not responsible for any of it. I know most of you were taught that if you don't feel for your sister, her children, etc., that you don't care. Perceivably, it feels good to feel empathy for your sister, for her children, and dance with them where they are at so that they feel that you love them and care for them. It all comes down to the same thing. What are you doing about it? Where are you invited in to have an impact with it? This is where you are playing with a beautiful, intimate relationship of the heart and letting it grow upon, grow upon and grow upon its self. From this place, the brother could share with his sister, "*I honor completely and totally, with all of my heart, where you are at here and what would you like to do about it?*" It is important to note that the brother is not coming from obligation nor seeing his sister as broken. He is coming from the love that he is, and that he can assist, as well as where she can go if she is willing.

So you are being the love that you are. You are so blessed to be able to assist other dear ones. Let's not underestimate how blessed you are that you **can** assist. A dear one is presenting right in front of you, the priceless beautiful gift that they are, and you have the priceless opportunity to assist these dear ones only because you can, and they have asked. You are not obligated. No one is broken. Where things get odd is if you come to this circumstance thinking that the dear one in front of you is broken. You are just so blessed that you can assist. It is your natural state to be able to assist. As no one is broken – then "*Wow, how best can we all complement the whole of humanity? Bring it on.*"

You can look further. How much satisfaction are you receiving just because you can assist another dear one, just because you can add to their journey? In truth, there is no satisfaction necessary nor gained, because there is no lack nor void within you that needs to be filled. Satisfaction is a whole lot different than feeling good and exuberant because you got to play with another life-stream around you. There is nothing you are seeking and there is everything that you are offering from a total and complete unanimous state of love.

William Linville – Universalis, Inc.
www.williamlinville.com

15476661R00070

Made in the USA
Middletown, DE
06 November 2014